A Visitor's Guide to Georgian England

A Visitor's Guide to Georgian England

Monica Hall

PEN & SWORD
HISTORY

First published in Great Britain in 2017 by
Pen & Sword History
an imprint of
Pen & Sword Books Ltd
47 Church Street
Barnsley
South Yorkshire
S70 2AS

ISBN 978 1 47387 685 9

A CIP catalogue record for this book is available from the British Library

Typeset in Ehrhardt by Mac Style Ltd, Bridlington, East Yorkshire

Printed and bound in Malta by Gutenberg Press Ltd.

Pen & Sword Books Ltd incorporates the imprints of Pen & Sword
Archaeology, Atlas, Aviation, Battleground, Discovery, Family History,
History, Maritime, Military, Naval, Politics, Railways, Select, Transport,
True Crime, Fiction, Frontline Books, Leo Cooper, Praetorian Press,
Seaforth Publishing and Wharncliffe.

For a complete list of Pen & Sword titles please contact
PEN & SWORD BOOKS LIMITED
47 Church Street, Barnsley, South Yorkshire, S70 2AS, England
E-mail: enquiries@pen-and-sword.co.uk
Website: www.pen-and-sword.co.uk

Contents

Chapter One

How to be a Georgian

S ince H.G. Wells wrote *The Time Machine* in 1895 people have dreamt of time-travelling, no matter that modern science raises some very trenchant objections to its possibility. It captures the modern imagination rather as Heaven did for our ancestors. Who has not day-dreamed about, say, nipping back to Tudor times to inform Henry VIII that it is the father who determines the gender of the baby? He wouldn't listen of course, and one would probably need a way of escaping back to the twenty-first century instantly to avoid the Tower, but that is not the point. Equally fascinating, and very problematic to the more thoughtful would-be time-traveller, are the consequences of interfering with history, as encapsulated by Zemeckis and Gale's 1985 film, *Back to the Future*. To do so might preclude the possibility of one's own birth, which would be the ultimate own goal.

I, personally, would like to spend some time among the Georgians. It seems to have been an era of considerable energy and optimism, combining scientific and philosophical progress with the sort of rather unruly social behaviour that we can only wistfully dream about today. We might not actually want to witness a public execution as they evidently did, but who has not secretly wanted to throw rotting fruit or vegetables at the sanctimonious people in public life who tell you what you should think, or how you should live? If you were a Georgian, you would have thrown it, had you had the opportunity. Forcefully.

Above all, the Georgians were optimistic risk-takers. They had to be, as there was no other way to live. They often did dangerous work in which the risk of tetanus or sepsis from wounds was ever present. The Industrial Revolution was underway, bringing both investment and employment opportunities – and the risk of losing money. Sanitation and drinking water was dubious to say the least, especially in towns and cities, and medical help were equally haphazard. Childbirth was still both inevitable and dangerous. But, most importantly, the Empire-builders were on the move.

As a nation, they were not faint-hearted. Those working for the East India Company faced a long and arduous journey in what we could consider ridiculously small and insanitary sailing ships, and when they got there they had to uphold the white man's burden by enduring tropical weather, parasites, and diseases – while persisting with absurdly unsuitable European clothing. Their womenfolk had to struggle to remain British household mistresses while contending with unfamiliar food, ailing children, inscrutable servants, and termites and mould attacking their homes. And they did, even though they had to face the 'deadly trinity of smallpox, cholera, and plague', and the fact that they died at twice the rate of fellow civil-servants in England. Unfortunate soldiers in the East India Company's 'private' armies died like flies. The Georgians, however, had a sense of opportunity and adventure that has evaporated since the vicissitudes of the twentieth century.

Today, one often feels that life in the West is a competition to see who can live the longest if one obsesses about diet, exercise, and a somewhat depressing level of self-denial, although nobody has yet convinced most of us that staggering into our late 90s is such a very good idea. The Georgians, who did not enjoy our life expectancy anyway, would have thought this a daft objective. Far better, they seem to have thought, to live hard and well in whatever time was available to them. Besides, the established religions that they were slowly coming to doubt did, at least, offer some redemption on their death-beds.

One real difference between the Georgians and their Stuart and Tudor ancestors, however, was the rationality of Enlightenment learning and thinking. Eighteenth century men (and women) really did pay considerable attention to the gaps in their traditional knowledge, and the scientific discoveries and philosophical thoughts emerging during their era. Largely, they seemed to have valued both thought and experience over superstition and undemocratic authority. This makes them modern indeed. In between such highbrow thoughts, however ... they liked to have *fun*, and this is their most endearing quality.

In order to understand the Georgians it is absolutely necessary to anchor their era in the context of what both went before, and came after, them. We can only but try to feel and understand the life and expectations of the eighteenth century. For the adventurous time-traveller, this book tries to offer an insight into their lives. They had great opportunities as well as considerable difficulties, and they obviously decided that the former should overcome the latter.

Anyone wanting to visit Georgian Britain might be rather surprised to find it relatively easy to fit in, because the Georgians, or at least those living in the cities, were rather familiar in their outlook and interests. Such an experience would depend, of course, on whether one were a man or a woman, and whether one were going to attempt to bluff it out in high society or virtuously empathise with life among the rural poor. Like most societies, the Georgians believed in equal opportunities for ordinary women when it came to doing the work and, although only men could do the heaviest jobs, the average woman would have had to be a lot tougher and physically stronger than most of us. At the beginning of the eighteenth century most people were working the land without the benefit of machinery or power. By the end of the eighteenth century, all this was in the throes of radical change.

But during the eighteenth century, the majority of the population was still mostly illiterate, somewhat superstitious, and beholden to employers or landlords. They were also subject to childhood diseases, and infections like tetanus and tuberculosis. Their diet, however, was not so very bad, especially compared to that of the poorer, and more numerous and urban, Victorians. It was probably neither as tasty nor exciting as ours, but more useful in terms of basic nutrition than we would generally suppose. A nourishing breakfast was often eschewed in humble households, due to practical reasons concerning dawn and the demands of livestock, but an early midday meal and a substantial supper were both absolutely necessary. The greatest responsibility of women was to ensure that the workers were well fed. Physically hard-working men needed at least four thousand+ calories a day, compared to our less than three thousand. Many of these calories were absorbed through bread, prepared in the local bakery, which has always been the human staple, together with rice in the Far East. Our ancestors knew the value of carbohydrates.

Despite their lack of education, however, some Georgians did display rather modern attitudes. Although outwardly religious, many were extremely suspicious of the relationship between the established Church of England and apparently heedless civil authority. The litany of organised Dissenters, from the seventeenth century Reformation onwards, is extraordinary. There were the Anabaptists, Behmenists, Diggers and Levellers, Grindletonians, Muggletonians, Ranters, Seekers – and many others. By Georgian times in England, however, it mainly came down to Methodists, Quakers, Baptists and Unitarians, who were known as 'rational dissenters'. They distrusted the established Church with its ritual and litany, were still religious, but believed that embracing the emerging knowledge of natural philosophy (science) might somehow endorse both their modern instincts and traditional beliefs.

These were people who could perhaps still recall times when their ancestors were horribly put to death for dissenting, or pursuing knowledge. Many of them were relatively poor, brave, and thinking people, who just knew that something was not quite fair when it came to their own relationship with religious worship and civil authority.

To understand just how these Georgians shaped our modern world and attitudes however, it would probably be best to land the time machine in London, among the better-off. Those who largely held the most power – cultural, intellectual, political, and financial.

There were, during the late eighteenth century, only about 5½ million people in England and Wales, and maybe another 1 million in Scotland. Remarkably, this population is also configured, but even rather less, in modern New Zealand. There were about 600,000 people in London in 1714, which is about the size of modern Sheffield. This is vastly smaller than now, but nonetheless quite impressive for 250 years ago when the whole of London town was barely larger than 3 square miles. However, by 1840, the environs of the capital would have expanded to accommodate nearly 2 million citizens.

The decades between the death of Queen Anne (1714) and 1830 encompassed much of the Enlightenment, and were times of great industrial, political, scientific, social and philosophical development, all of which fuelled the growth of the British Empire. This, in turn, led to the rise of Britain as the world leader in Victorian times. Apologists for the Empire often refer to the dastardly English, but this is quite wrong, as any historically-aware Scotsman, Irishman or Welshman could tell you. They were all in it together, especially the Scots; for better, and not for worse. Dr Samuel Johnson, who detested the Scots, despite claiming to have spent a lifetime trying to like them, famously remarked that 'The noblest prospect which a Scotsman ever sees, is the high road that leads him to England.' It is interesting that few of the many eminent eighteenth century Scots seem to have disagreed with him, at least in practical, if not in cultural, terms.

It is impossible to isolate any main driver of Britain's eighteenth century development because each contributed to a positive feedback loop which enhanced progress in other areas. Philosophy, during the Enlightenment, encouraged free-thinking, reduced dependence upon the Church for answers to difficult questions, and invigorated both science and the arts. Industrial and mechanical advances, mathematics, and chemical discoveries, fostered the development of natural philosophy as an experimental discipline, and made possible the adoption of careful data analysis as a source of hypothesis, experimentation, and progress. Prior to that, the arrival on the throne of a reluctant non-English-speaking Hanoverian, in the shape of George I, must have made the ascendance of the House of Commons, and democracy, rather easier. The media was also changing rapidly. Though still only the preserve of the literate, improved technology spread ideas and, worse, irreverence towards the ruling classes. The 'modern' cartoon was born in the eighteenth century, as was satire and, suddenly, the great and the good had to beware of ridicule, much to the probable delight of the nation. It was a perfect storm, and one which we should recognise since we are in the midst of an Internet-driven information revolution which bears many philosophical and practical similarities.

The Georgians undoubtedly enjoyed their liberty in a freer social culture, but they had not anticipated the industrial change that would be brought about by the progress of science and mechanisation in their lifetime. In the eighteenth century everything began to change considerably. This is a situation that we should understand; the replacement of less efficient human labour by mechanisation or, in our case now, robotics or artificial intelligence. Human redundancy is a fearful consequence for most people.

The time traveller will find many similarities between the Georgians and us, but modern democracy, social sensitivity, and risk-assessment are not among them. This may partly be because the Georgians were not enfranchised. Only about 200,000 men were rich and influential enough to have the vote, and many MPs represented 'rotten boroughs' in which only a handful of men had a disproportionate representation in Parliament. None of this was lost on ordinary people, nor among the media commentators who wrote and drew for the ever-growing market of political pamphlets, books, newspapers, and ballads. Most working people might not have been able to read very well, or indeed at all, but they did love a cartoon and a song. The powerful had to put up with being bullied, ridiculed, and unmercifully satirised in print, and reputations could both rise and fall very rapidly. One contemporary aspect of all this, with which we would instantly empathise, is the gradual drain of entitlement and self-confidence among those accustomed to rule. Their natural authority was beginning to ebb away. In previous centuries such impudence might have had very dire consequences, but the Enlightenment and increased literacy was working its magic. There was still an astonishing number of crimes for which the death penalty was available, even though it was carried out far less frequently than we suppose, but being disrespectful to one's betters was no longer one of them.

In fact, being merely disrespected was the least of the problems that royalty, the government, and the great and the good, had to face. They had to put up with scurrilous and irrefutable slander and libel, against which any legal remedy was feeble, to say the very least. A twenty-first century time-traveller might find this rather invigorating, at least for a while, given that we are circumscribed almost to the point of muteness. The Georgians would be very scornful of such a notion as they were breathing the heady air of freedom of speech – if not the equality and protection of citizens which we now take for granted – theoretically, at least. They were among the forerunners of modern justice and equality, even though they might not have quite realised that potential in themselves. They were the first to successfully exploit the media as a vehicle for promoting social and governmental change.

When not fretting or scoffing about their betters and rulers however, Britons knew that their country really was a land of unfettered opportunity, one aspect of which is reflected in the amount of building in London in both the public and private sectors.

Richard Blome's map of 1673 shows a large town in which London's West End is just beginning to be developed, but it is chiefly distinguished by the amount of arable or swampy land very close by, especially south of the river. John Rocque's famous 24-sheet map of 1746 shows the development over seventy-odd years. This development was not, of course, mere haphazard expansion. It also involved the considerable redevelopment of existing medieval areas, drainage, the building of the many Georgian terraces that we now so cherish, and great public works. One enthusiast was the neo-classicist and somewhat eccentric architect Sir John Soane (1753–1837), whose museum in Lincoln's Inn Fields is one of London's hidden gems. His extant (though sometimes re-modelled) works include the Bank of England, the Royal Chelsea Hospital, the Dulwich Picture Gallery and the Freemasons' Hall. It is true that much of the building took place in the Regency era, but it all began some time before that. Before twentieth/twenty-first century gentrification, many Georgian terraces had descended from middle-class aspiration to Victorian slums, due to the huge influx of the poor into London, in search of work and betterment after 1830. Such buildings began, however, as residences for the burgeoning Georgian middle classes. Here again, one finds many similarities with the twenty-first century. Georgian terraces were often rather jerry-built, as gentrification has laid bare, and many people did comparatively little cooking, being very fond of fast-food take-away meals. It all sounds strangely familiar.

Of course, for any time-traveller from the twenty-first century, the most ghastly consequences will probably be physical; health, hygiene, and childbirth. It was, naturally, entirely expected that the poor would succumb to such horrors on a regular basis, so it is useful to linger among the better-off and discover how they began to improve matters, eventually for all of us. Many 'discoveries' of the eighteenth century were, in fact, known to others but, due to poor communications, they had to wait upon later European scholarship for general renown and development. The Turks, for example, had been inoculating their children against smallpox for some considerable time before Edward Jenner (1749–1823), used live virus and a needle, and with considerable success and far fewer deaths. How very lucky for us that it happened in 1796, and that we do not have to face up to such medical ethical dilemmas as trying out one's theories on a small boy, or even oneself. In fact, much of what we now know, understand and pursue to our own advantage, is the direct descendant of unregulated, and unethical, eighteenth to mid-twentieth century science.

If I were to advocate a modern phrase to guide you as you pass some time among your Georgian forebears, it would be 'Go for it!' They would have both understood and liked that.

So let's go Georgian, and shed some preconceptions about our own scientific progress and knowledge. After all, it is only about sixty-five years since the radio space-traveller hero Buck Rogers memorably bawled at his crew to 'throw some more uranium on the boiler', and that was post Second World War. We need to take a journey through the lives of the Georgian movers and shakers, and the ordinary people. Their aspirations; their family, social, working and political networks; how science and technology changed their lives and hopes and, of course, how they had fun.

First, however, you must be suitably dressed if you hope to deceive anyone into leaving you alone to venture forth from your lodgings, and prowl around to find out exactly what Georgian England was like.

Chapter Two

Clothes & Beauty

'Clothes make the man. Naked people have little or no influence on society.'
Mark Twain (1835–1910)

The first requirement for the time-traveller is to blend into the background, and that will mean looking the part, so a visit to Angels, the legendary London theatrical costumiers, might be necessary before departure. With their help, you could hope to pass muster as either an aristocrat or a pauper, although you would undoubtedly smell far too clean. For a while, at any rate.

Apart from perhaps thongs and killer heels, those of us in the twenty-first century are accustomed to thinking that our clothes should be reasonably comfortable. This will not be the case in fashionable Georgian circles when clothes and beauty, for both sexes, involved both discomfort and inconvenience. This did not go unnoticed at the time, with jeering cartoonists lampooning the ultra-fashionable young Macaronis, more about whom later.

Everyone else got away with being far less ridiculous of course, but there is no doubt that appearance was very important among the fashionable and aspiring. As, indeed, it still is today, but undoubtedly less restricting or even dangerous. '*Il faut souffrir pour être belle*' is an aphorism which spread here from eighteenth century France, but was also widely observed in much earlier societies, and means 'One must suffer for beauty.' They certainly did, as had many others before them, and since. The Georgians, given their capacity for risk-taking and sheer expenditure in the pursuit of physical attraction, would have been queueing up for Botox, plastic surgery, implants, veneers, hair extensions and gym membership, had it been possible. As it is, they did their best to subvert the unfairness of time and Nature with their own versions of our beauty interventions, and probably just admired each other's efforts rather more than the actual results.

Given that, in the eighteenth century, it was rather easier for the aspiring to dress the part, rather than radically change one's physical attributes, clothes will be considered first.

Georgian era clothes changed very considerably over the years between the accession of George I (1714) to the death of George IV (1830). The immediate precursor was the baroque period, which is defined as dating from about 1650, and embraced not only changes in the design of clothes but also in architecture, art and music. Baroque fashion in Europe was most influenced by the royal family and wealthy courtiers at the Court of the Sun King, Louis XIV (1638–1715) at Versailles. The reputation of Parisian couturiers, which endures to this day, was well and truly established after Louis certified the establishment of a guild of dressmakers, embracing both men and women designers, who must rank among the earliest and canniest of 'modern' marketers. These people understood the importance of ever-changing designs for their richest clients, the trickle-down effects of the bourgeoisie aping their betters, and the financial opportunities as the former tried to play catch-up, whilst the rich were determined to deny lesser (and scorned) mortals any such chance. They established the principles of market segmentation, differential pricing policy, and built-in product obsolescence, and they skilfully exploited it.

To understand exactly how canny were these clothes designers, it is necessary to take a closer look at both the clothes designs they inherited, and the legacy they left the Georgians.

Charles II (1630–1685), 'The Merry Monarch', was a very keen consumer of extravagant baroque clothing, as befits his reputation as a ladies' man. He had, of course, been brought up in fashionable Europe after the age of 14 when he fought alongside his father, and was then obliged to flee. His father, Charles I was executed by the Parliamentarians in 1649, and was usually painted wearing a seventeenth-century-style *piccadill* ruff. After the Restoration, Charles II favoured big wigs, ruffles, tricorn hats, and extravagantly embroidered, but co-ordinated, coats and breeches. This was the genesis of the modern suit, known to the French in the eighteenth century as the 'suite'. It is interesting to note here that the women's baroque clothing was not designed to encourage rapid movement or, indeed, anything beyond being sedately decorative. The gentlemen, on the other hand, were free to stride around, even if somewhat encumbered by swords and wigs.

One of the most distinctive aspects was the display of a gentleman's calf in tights below knee breeches. This appears to have been both alluring to women and a symbol of powerful masculinity to other men, and endured until the demise of breeches in favour of trousers in the nineteenth century. This was true only if you had a good calf, of course; a man with a weedy calf must have suffered considerably in terms of self-esteem. This was not new, of course, as anyone familiar with the portraits of Henry VIII and his son, Edward VI, in their 'power poses' will know. The key to masculine approval until the late eighteenth century was muscularity, which led to some rather strange depictions of obviously obese, rakish, or elderly gentlemen who were still apparently sporting a relatively comely calf, as can be seen in cartoons of the Prince Regent as drawn by Gillray for example. George IV's physical shortcomings, including his congested facial complexion and drunken eyes, receive no mercy at all … except for his calf muscles, even if they have to be sufficiently stout to support all that dissolute fat. Rumour had it, though, that George bulked out his calves with prosthetics for public appearances, so iconic were a man's lower legs.

There were cartoons in which a victim's pitiful calf was exaggerated to add to the satirical effect. Gillray drew a very weedy Prime Minister, William Pitt the Younger, bursting in to break bad news about the Swedish royal family to King George III and Queen Charlotte. Neither of whom are kindly depicted, on their shared commode, both looking irredeemably stupid, and nothing like monarchs. The imputation was that the shooting of the Swedish king was a much better laxative for the constipated king than any medicine could be.

Baroque clothes left a clear legacy for both the Georgians, the Victorians and us, as the gentlemen's suit gradually began to evolve. Beginning as a fashion extravaganza in the baroque period, the 'suite' became a statement of power and authority as it became more stylized and less frivolous over the decades, and dark and staid clothing was good for those involved in trade and finance, or intellectual pursuits, as it denoted seriousness and reliability. It also conferred status, as black clothing demanded much more dye to be suitably dense, and was thus relatively expensive. Poorer people wore clothes of a beige or natural hue. Religion was also inextricably involved in clothing, and the rise of European Protestantism from the sixteenth century onwards favoured dour apparel and covered hair for the faithful, and demonized the more colourful garb of Catholic ceremony as evidence of vanity; one of the seven deadly sins. Our relatively minimalist cathedrals and churches which we so revere today, were once, before the Reformation, a riot of painted saints meeting horrible ends on the walls, gilded pillars, and stained-glass windows. These depictions were well-known religious stories which the faithful poor could contemplate in peace while the priest droned on in Latin, which they could not understand anyway.

In Tudor times, people were subject to the sumptuary laws, which were designed to restrict 'unsuitable' consumption, keep them in their place, and make that place immediately obvious to everyone. They were also a barrier to the importation of foreign textiles which would have been in direct economic competition with domestic production. Of a staggering attention to detail, these laws dictated the fabric, style, colour and construction of permissible clothes, the number of courses and comestibles one could eat at dinner, and the style of one's furniture. They were a complex and forensic dissection of both class and income. There was nothing new about this, as such laws had been enacted around the known world from at least the times of classical Greece, and probably before, especially in China.

However, as the burgeoning British Empire began to take shape in the seventeenth century, and entrepreneurial talent began to be needed no matter where it came from, such laws necessarily fell into abeyance and, finally, into desuetude in the reign of James I. Old money might prefer to do business and socialise with their peers but, when it came to new opportunity and real money, all bets were off. An adventurous and rapacious sea captain might be in no way a gentleman, but if he could deliver to your family a sugar estate in the West Indies with slave labour from Africa, then so be it. After all, few beneficiaries at the top of the slave-trade food-chain had ever seen an African, a slave ship, or personally met the obliging sea captains, or the managers and overseers of their Caribbean estates. And those (probably younger sons) who were sent out to keep the family fortunes on track, probably did not divulge the ways in which this was achieved. At least, certainly not to the women in the family, whose opinion usually did not count in any case. Sugar was the oil of the eighteenth century.

By Georgian times, thus, upward mobility was signalled and achieved by one's address, conspicuous consumption, and clothing. Not so very different to our times, indeed.

Freedom of physical movement in Georgian clothing tended to depend upon class. The higher up the social scale you were, the more difficult things became, in practical terms, and the more you were dressed for social recognition and esteem, especially if you were a woman. Rather like the Chinese emperors who allegedly grew their fingernails to huge length in order to impress upon the peasantry that they did not have to work, the Georgian aristocracy wore clothes we would regard as depressingly difficult. In fact most women were expected to wear a cap, long skirts, and some sort of stays, if they wanted to be regarded as 'respectable', even when toiling (often pregnant) in agriculture, or for the nascent Industrial Revolution in small factories. We are familiar with women and children working in poor conditions in Victorian times, thanks to the books, newspapers and magazines of the media, and the explosion of social conscience and consequent labour laws, but such labour was pre-dated by at least 100 years. Entrepreneurs, then as now, knew that the key to profit and expansion was mechanization and cheap labour.

The emerging factory system of the eighteenth century grew out of the domestic system, in which workers used hand tools in their own homes or workshops in order to produce, for example, textiles or ceramics. The growth of water, and then steam power meant, however, that engineers could develop systems of mass production which meant that labour had to be concentrated outside the home and in factories. Factory-owners employed just about anyone from a very early age, but women and children were liked because they were cheaper, nimble, and more biddable, and only a relatively high-earning man could afford to keep his wife at home and his children in education. It must have seemed an economic opportunity for poor families, but it came at a very high price in terms of disease and accidents, and many of the latter were caused by the totally unsuitable clothing the women wore to work. Long, voluminous skirts and unstoppable machinery were not a happy mix.

However, although the lives of the poor will be considered in more detail later, it is probably better to be a rather wealthier time traveller to begin with, to actually see how Georgian society and industry worked from the top down. Thus, for the moment, it will be assumed that the problems of getting dressed and fitting-in are somewhat more concerned with social acceptance among the better-off.

It would be better for both aristocratic and aspirational Georgians, of either gender, to get dressed before applying their heavy and very unsubtle make-up, to avoid soiling the extravagant clothes, which were not easy to clean, even with the aid of servants. This involved layer upon layer of natural fibres – cotton, wool and silk. It is entirely possible that the chilliness of the northern European temperate climate and housing favoured bulky clothes, but fashion and public display were probably the dictators. Indeed, European fashion persisted even when it was wildly unsuited to the climes, with Empire-building British gentlemen wearing heavy clothes suitable to their status. Any deviation from such crazy attire was viewed, very gravely, as 'going native'. The wives of East India Company administrators and nascent colonialists had to endure wigs, layers and stays (corsets) in the tropical heat not only because it denoted status, but because it also meant that native men would be less likely to show an interest in such bewilderingly iron-clad women. Or so their husbands hoped. In desperation, however, the sweating and fainting pioneers found ways to cheat by dispensing with linings in coats, jackets and waistcoats, multiple undergarments, or only struggling into the stays for public occasions. And some lonely ladies, whilst their husbands were touring the vastness of their purviews for months on end, regrettably turned their eyes towards their handsome servants.

Back in London, however, there were no such excuses for not sticking to the dictates of fashion. So, let's get dressed, Georgian-style. Ladies first.

For centuries women have been wearing garments designed to enhance, support or conceal their breasts, which seem to have veered between the flat-chested gamine and the voluptuous décolletage, according to the fashion of the times. Often, remarkably, in the same woman. The Georgians celebrated uplift and cleavage for glamorous evening occasions, but generally favoured a more modest approach to the bosom otherwise. Before the twentieth-century brassiere, uplift and cleavage was achieved with the stays (prototype corset) as, indeed, was flattening. It was not, however, the first garment to be donned when getting dressed. This may have been because it would have left unsightly traces of the uncompromising stiffening structures and laces on the skin, or more probably because it was easier to launder camisoles than stays. Whatever the reason, the ladies dressed in cotton undergarments before the imprisoning stays. There were no buttons on ladies' garments, and the stability of the many layers depended upon tapes, loops, and alarmingly long pins that were anchored into the stays. The button is hardly modern, believed as it is to date back 5,000 years to the Indus Valley, but it seems to have been one of those concepts which begins as purely functional and is then strangely subverted into the decorative. Buttons were certainly in evidence in the eighteenth century, but mostly uselessly adorning men's open coats, and not assisting the ladies with their fiddlesome garments.

Stays were equated with morals and respectability in the eighteenth century, and any woman not so buttressed would have been considered as loose. In his *Rake's Progress*, Hogarth's somewhat dishevelled prostitute's profession is signalled by the absence of stays, and also the number of oddly-placed beauty spots on her face that conceal her syphilitic sores.

Here is a basic tutorial on how to get dressed, and it will not be a rapid procedure for the middle-class or aristocratic novice:

- ✓ Summon your ladies' maid, if you have one;
- ✓ Wash hands, face, under-arms and feet in the hot water provided by her; immersion bathing is a much more occasional and major event requiring considerable preparation, and is also considered rather dangerous. Your scented soda and olive oil soap will be a valuable domestic commodity and, by the late eighteenth century, rather less unappealing than earlier versions made of wood ash, lye, and animal fats;
- ✓ Clean your teeth, probably with alum and a sponge;
- ✓ Put on the knee-length light cotton camisole or shift, which probably has three-quarter length sleeves, over which –
- ✓ Struggle into the stays which will control your bosom and stomach, and be laced either to front or back. Tuck in the tapes;
- ✓ Clamber into the knitted stockings, and the tie garters which support them just above the knee. Try not to worry unduly about varicose veins;
- ✓ Begin on the petticoats, but bear in mind that you might want to in-corporate a bustle, 'bum roll', hip pads, or hoops between the layers, which will need to be secured by tapes. Tuck in the tapes again;
- ✓ Don the 'fichu'; a modest and decorative shawl-like garment covering the bare shoulders and the bosom, and tuck the ends into the petti-coats;
- ✓ After at least two, or maybe more, petticoats, you can get into your gown, which is often rather more like a coat and is made of the most glamorous and colourful material you can afford, and fastens at the front bodice; the matching or contrasting top 'petticoat' will be visi-ble at the lower front, and you may want to add a stomacher;
- ✓ Firmly anchor the gown to your stays at the front with the long and worrying pins;
- ✓ Apply make-up as appropriate to your status, and it will not be subtle since a densely white complexion with round red cheeks was consid-ered attractive. If you are masquerading as a 'painted' society aristo-crat you will also need red lip stain, dark brows, and a beauty spot;
- ✓ No woman in the eighteenth century got away without a cap, hat, bonnet, and elaborate hairdo or wig, depending on her status, the time of day or the occasion, and here the hairdressing skills of your maid will come into their own. Whatever status you aspire to, tum-

bling locks are not appropriate in respectable women beyond early adolescence;

✓ You will need some jewellery, and delicate shoes to peep out from beneath the gown and petticoats indoors. Georgian women often wore sensible boots outside, especially if they could not afford a sedan chair, to avoid the mud and ordure in the streets;

✓ Sweep down into Society, knowing full well that the stockings will be constantly creeping down and that the pins will need regular adjustment or re-anchoring if they are not to jab you in the ribs.

Nobody contemplated knickers for women until the late eighteenth century and, at first, they were considered the preserve of 'fast' women, which is slightly odd, except that the concept rather drew attention to a woman's most intimate area. One might think that was because, given the layers of undergarments and long skirts, nobody's modesty was likely to be compromised by a sudden updraft. Or, possibly, that pulling things down as well as lifting them up was just too much of a performance when relieving oneself, especially given Georgian lavatorial arrangements. The Georgians, of necessity, were not shy about the call of nature and in public places the upper-class ladies sometimes discretely used a porcelain potty, called a bourdaloue, for urination, which resembled a gravy-boat. Anecdote has it that God-fearing ladies took these to church with them in order to last through the inordinately long and, usually depressing, sermons. What became of the contents of the bourdaloue after the service does not seem to be recorded. One suspects they were surreptitiously emptied in the churchyard by a maid. They were also used in other public places, like theatres, although it seems certain that the ladies retreated away from the public eye when necessity called.

The palace of Versailles, just outside Paris, was notorious for fantastic luxury marred by heaps of ordure dotted in corners around its miles of corridors. Such behaviour was not condoned, but given the many hundreds of courtiers and servants, untrained dogs, and insufficient commodes, the palace and gardens descended into filth. Horace Walpole (1717–1797) and various ambassadors complained about the stench long after Louis XIV declared that the hallways should be cleaned (once a week). Of course, it is easy for us to blench now, with our lavatories and sewer systems, for which we have to thank the Victorians who realised that poor domestic hygiene was, indeed, a social problem of huge consequences. The Georgians, however, did their best given their technological shortcomings, and were not unaware of the problems. They just didn't have the solutions.

However, returning to the fashionable at the eighteenth century court of Louis XVI and Marie-Antoinette, the ladies were required to execute an extraordinary method of locomotion now called the 'Versailles Glide', which effectively vetoed the normal bouncy walk of a physically-fit woman. It has been speculated that it was developed to avoid stepping on the train of the lady in front, which seems somewhat unlikely as it would have been much easier just to leave a larger gap between the processing ladies. However, given that nearly every aspect of behaviour was either prescribed, or proscribed, at Versailles, it may possibly be true. If Marie-Antoinette was adept at this excruciating method of getting around at Court then it is certain that the other ladies would have learned to do the same, and would have been encouraged to emulate the queen by their ambitious husbands or fathers. Foreign diplomats, including the often-visiting Horace Walpole, described the spectacle as ladies rolling down the corridors, as if on wheels. Such a trick would be aided by the underwear frameworks of the huge skirts fashionable at the time, known in France as *grand panniers* (big baskets), which would conceal the footwork. Some modern women, historians or dance teachers, have attempted to reproduce the Versailles Glide, with mixed results. They argue whether or not the ball of the foot would have stayed on the ground, resulting in a sort of shuffle, or whether the steps were so tiny as to be imperceptible. They nearly all agree, however, that the strain on the bent knees, lower leg muscles, rigidly imprisoned spines (by stays), and the sheer weight of clothing, would have made this an agonising fashionable imposition. One can imagine that upper-class Chinese women, whose feet had been bound from infancy rendering them effectively disabled, would have empathized with the victims of such a strange imperative. It never caught on here.

So much for the ladies.

Getting dressed was not that much easier for Georgian men. Long before the dissolute and overweight 'Prinny' became Regent, upper-class men had been cramming their bulging figures into stays and other supremely uncomfortable clothes for the sake of vanity, even if they were not Macaronis. A 'Macaroni', the eighteenth century precursor to the nineteenth century rather tougher 'dandy', was a somewhat effeminate follower of fashion, who took it to noteworthy levels in terms of dress, wigs, lifestyle, and slang. The term still survives in the American folk song 'Yankee Doodle Went to Town', the state anthem of Connecticut.

The Macaronis were some of the wealthy young men who returned from their (supposedly educational) Grand Tour with absurdly extravagant Continental fashion ideas and language, and a taste for pasta dishes. One supposes this was a form of youthful rebellion, and that it would have been just as annoyingly successful, say, as the son of an Archbishop becoming a Goth today. By the late eighteenth century, however, it had all got a bit too much. The imputation of effeminacy and the attendant public ridicule was a major drawback, as was the sheer cost and time involved, and one imagines that the commitment needed to endure the physical discomfort of wearing idiotic clothes and balancing enormous wigs must have waned. By the Regency, an inevitable backlash began to see even fashionable men re-claiming their masculinity, dispensing with the wigs and make-up and, even, cultivating facial hair; 'the great masculine renunciation' (Laughran, 2003). One can scarcely imagine later fictional heroes such as Darcy, Rochester or Heathcliff, for example, messing around with wigs and make-up. The abandonment of men's wigs also received a fillip from one of those ill-conceived taxes which politicians often think are a good idea at the time. In 1795, in order to raise revenue, a tax was imposed on wig powder by William Pitt. This, however, failed spectacularly as people promptly either stopped wearing powdered wigs, or used flour, and the tax raised only 46,000 guineas. What is the modern day equivalent?

Some gentlemen, however, remained rather touchy about their silhouettes, and stays and corsets for them were rather more widespread than is generally supposed. One can see how eighteenth-century men's underwear addressed at least two of their main preoccupations; those of a youthful figure ... and virility. A cartoon of the time shows a hopeful expression on the face of a gentleman who is being tight-laced by his (much smaller, of course) servant. Both have weedy calves and ridiculous shoes.

Men's clothes during the eighteenth century were mostly variations upon a theme of 'stockings', shirt, waistcoat, below-the-knee breeches, band-collar, stock or cravat, and top coat. Until the end of the century, clothes tended to be tight-fitting but, at least, were rather easier to wear than the copious coat skirts and cuffs of the Baroque period. Wigs were usually reserved for evenings or formal gatherings and, if long, were tied at the back, or if shorter resembled the wigs still seen today on barristers' heads in court. Gentlemen's day coats, without which no well-dressed man would be seen, were usually made of plain cloth, and long to the knee. Fashionable Georgian men were enthusiastic about colour because, apart from being cheerful, dyes were expensive and evidence of status even if dense black carried similar connotations, for different lifestyles. Formal coats were distinguished from day coats by both hue, and decoration at the edges and on pockets. Waistcoats were the item of clothing which were often the most extravagant and luxurious. Long walking canes seem to have been a fashionable accessory, albeit without practical function for most normally fit men and, were possibly, rather more an aid to swaggering.

Beauty

For fashionable Georgian women and men, make-up was indispensable and was, basically, the art of deception as much as enhancement. Youth and natural beauty was much admired in both sexes of course, but sadly it did not endure, as so many writers over the millennia have observed with a sigh. Among the poor, hard physical labour, constant childbirth, and disease, combined to make the golden days of youth rather short-lived. By the eighteenth century the epidemic of smallpox was at its height, and even healthy adults were also very susceptible to blood poisoning from accidents, wounds and tooth abscesses.

The Romantics (circa 1770–1848) rhapsodized over naturally-lovely young girls, of course, but only a decade or two after fashionable and cosmetic eighteenth century excesses:

> And on that cheek, and o'er that brow,
> So soft, so calm, yet eloquent,
> The smiles that win, the tints that glow,
> But tell of days in goodness spent,
> A mind at peace with all below,
> A heart whose love is innocent!
> 'She Walks in Beauty', Byron (1788–1824)

The Romantics, who included Byron and Mary Shelley were intellectual throw-backs to medieval times, rather than the Greek or Latin classical eras. Emotion, individualism, and glorification of the past and nature figured large in their writings, rather than modern philosophy as represented by such luminaries as Hobbes, Locke, Hume, Payne or Immanuel Kant.

Not everyone was fooled by the image of beauty however, and the fear of entrapment by make-up was so widespread that Parliament was obliged to pass an Act in 1770 which stated that:

> ... all women, of whatever age, rank, profession or degree, whether virgins, maids or widows, that shall, from and after such Act, impose upon, seduce or betray into matrimony, any of His Majesty's subjects, by the scents, paints, cosmetic washes, artificial teeth, false hair, Spanish wool, iron stays, hoops, high-heeled shoes, bolstered hips, shall incur the penalty of the law in force against witchcraft and like misdemeanours and that the marriage upon conviction shall stand null and void.

This list of proscribed artifices makes the tutorial above on how to get dressed seem rather unexceptional and pedestrian. To be fair to Lord Byron, he was writing after the most extraordinary excesses of Georgian self-adornment had been replaced by somewhat less wild fashions and, indeed, his appreciation of his lovely young lady may have owed a good deal to both the 1770 Act, Pitt's 1795 hair powder tax, and the French Revolution, which understandably reduced the popularity of wearing ostentatious wigs among the aristocracy both in France and in the nearby, and nervous, UK. Thomas Rowlandson's 1792 *Six Stages of Mending a Face* (clockwise from the left) splendidly illustrated just how bad things could be, and was rather ambiguously dedicated to the Rt. Hon. Lady Archer. Her response, if any, is not recorded.

None of this was new, of course. In England, since Tudor times at least, women had been resorting to artifice to disguise the ravages of diet, disease, and time. By the time she died in 1603, aged 68, Queen Elizabeth I was nearly bald and pock-marked, and was in the grip of grotesque cosmetics. She also allegedly conformed to an English fashion of 'extreme cleavage'. The French Ambassador remarked, somewhat startled, that she was sometimes to be seen in Court virtually bare-bosomed. It has to be remembered, though, that French ambassadors have not always been reliable witnesses when it comes to describing the English and their monarchs and habits.

The growing fondness for 'white gold' (sugar) played havoc with the teeth of the Georgians who could afford it, and the aspirational even thought that blackened teeth were something to be proud of since they denoted wealth. Smallpox left scarring, and venereal disease was often signalled to the observant by significant hair loss. Pepys wrote in the seventeenth century, somewhat unfeelingly, about the shame he felt about his syphilitic brother's sparse pate, although one cannot help but feel sympathy for those who were suffering from premature baldness for innocent genetic reasons. However, the wig provided a solution for that, and no doubt hawk-eyed observers could tell the difference between natural male-pattern baldness and the tufts and gaps which indicated a rather less innocent reason for hair loss.

When it came to make-up, the Georgian preference was for ghostly whiteness, both in wigs and on the faces of the fashionable of both sexes, and the liberal powdering of both was *de rigeur* amongst the well to-do. Some ingredients were innocent enough, such as flour or chalk, but others certainly were not. Still in use in Georgian times, although its detrimental effects must have been suspected at least, was lead in face powder. The unappetising recipes also included vinegar, extract of horse manure, and (presumably strong) perfume. As a contrast to the desired pallor, both sexes used carmine rouge on their cheeks, and not subtly; to our minds, they would have looked like Dutch dolls. Wigs needed something to stick the whitening powder in place, and that something was lard. When wigs went out of fashion, they used flour on their own hair rather than pay Walpole's tax. At least, one supposes, it might have suffocated the ubiquitous head lice.

It was not until the time of Jane Austen that the more natural look for both sexes became more fashionable and men could be reasonably sure that, come the wedding night, they were not in for a dreadful shock and the need to resort to the courts to get their marriage annulled. The girls of marriageable age also benefited from the men's retreat from wigs and artifice, but probably not because men had decided that they should play fair. It seems more to have been an issue of masculinity, because the Macaronis had got everyone nervous about being labelled effeminate.

So who, in such times, made these cosmetics?

The notion of non-industrial cosmetic production actually survives until the 1870s and beyond. Industrial production certainly became possible, thanks to Max Factor (b. 1872) and others in the early twentieth century, largely due to the nascent movie industry. But people 100 years earlier still relied upon themselves, or their local apothecary, who had a recipe book for drugs, cosmetics, pest extermination, inks, domestic cleaning compounds, perfumes etc., the forerunner of the *Pharmaceutical Formulas* (first edition 1898). Brush or finger-applied lipsticks date from possibly 5,000 years ago and from the Middle Ages onwards included such exotic (or off-putting) ingredients as pig fats, gold leaf, animal marrow, the ubiquitous carmines, and fish scales for that alluring glittery look.

Meanwhile, in the eighteenth century, women were still busy making cosmetics themselves. Hannah Glasse, of the cookery book reknown (1784), included recipes for soaps, tooth powder, perfumes, and other beauty aids. However, the chemists were beginning to understand that some cosmetics were lethal or, at the least, very detrimental to health, and in the nineteenth century scientists began to proscribe some ingredients. They were not very happy about lead or arsenic (for facial preparations) and belladonna (for alluringly large pupils), but in Georgian times any such preparations bought from an apothecary might well contain these alarming ingredients. Lead attacks the bodies and brains of the young particularly, but it took into the twentieth century for its use to be regulated. In 2007, the US authorities discovered that 70 per cent of lipsticks contained lead, and some in amounts which might be beyond safe levels if the wearer was in the habit of applying it three or more times a day and then ingesting it by licking it off. Arsenic and belladonna are virulent poisons, of course, but so great is the human desire to improve upon nature that the use of these dangerous concoctions persisted well into the nineteenth century, despite the objections of scientists and doctors.

You can still make your own beauty aids (and not die as a result) although some hardly sound subtle. The mascaras sound frankly eye-watering, being made of soap and lamp-black.

HANNAH GLASSE'S GEORGIAN COLD CREAM
One pint of trotter-oil, a quarter-pound of hog's lard, one ounce of spermaceti, a bit of virgin-wax; warm them together with a bit of rose water, and beat it up with a whisk.

VICTORIAN FACE BEAUTIFIER
Syrupy lactic acid 40 oz., Glycerine 80 oz., Tincture of benzoin 3 oz., Carmine No. 40 40 gr., Ammonia solution 0.5 oz., Water 3 oz., perfume.

WIG PASTE
For fastening the wig to the head.
Isinglass (fish glue) 1 part, Rose water 8 parts, Tincture of benzoin 2 parts, Oil of Turpentine 2 parts, Alcohol 4 parts.

Much has been speculated about the sheer smelliness of Georgians given their reluctance to immerse themselves in a bath, the sheer difficulty of cleaning clothes, and dearth of efficient drain systems and clean domestic water. There is however, no real reason to suppose that they did not frequently wash themselves in better-off households. Our modern air-conditioned, tobacco-free, deodorised, anti-bacterial, and 'fragranced' life is a very recent phenomenon. Anyone born before about 1950 will know perfectly well that any bus, cinema or the London Underground, for example, reeked of tobacco, sweat, and damp coats and hair. But if everyone is involved in contributing to such a miasma, then nobody notices so very much, although the Georgian city aroma will certainly present a problem to the fastidious twenty-first century time-traveller. The outdoor privy was a comparative luxury for a well-off family, and the poor had to contend with the common privy. Neither were connected to any system of flushing or drainage, and nightsoil men carted away the malodorous remains … at least once every six months. Many of these cesspools, in poor districts, were merely in the basements of the houses. It was also thought a good idea to line the basements with porous bricks, so that much of the detritus might just seep away. However, this resulted in unsuspected and dire consequences as the effluvia affected sources of domestic water. So, no matter how wealthy the society you might choose to live in during your Georgian adventure, you will be at risk from stench and disease due to a lack of hygiene and understanding.

You will also be confronted with lice, fleas, bed-bugs and ticks, as there will be no sure way to avoid these parasites, no matter how wealthy. Georgian bodies, wigs, clothes and beds were havens for such creatures. Your sixty-four great-great-great-great grandparents, some of whose names you may actually know from Internet genealogy sites, undoubtedly endured such pests as a fact of life, and took their presence for granted, no matter how rich or poor. The wealthier, of course, made considerable efforts to banish from their lives such infernal nuisances but, unfortunately, it did not always go well for the humans, involving as it did some seriously dangerous poisons and practices. Insects are rather robust when it comes to annihilation, given their massive reproductive capacities, whereas human beings are not. People suffered as a result of inhaling or ingesting poisons designed to eliminate the pests in their houses, whereas the insects often just carried on as usual, little troubled by a slight diminution of their many offspring. It would, incidentally, certainly be most advisable *not* to hire a wig.

The Georgians also had to contend with large numbers of mice and rats. That they were after the humans' food supplies is obvious, of course, but they also damaged clothes as mice, especially, liked to chew them up and make nests in them. One solution might be to keep cats, but this was easier said than done in Georgian times when there was no cat litter or neutering. Most cats then lived a feral or semi-feral life, rather than being beloved and pampered pets and, as any cat-owner will know, if the duty of the cat is to kill house mice they have to be kept hungry, and persuaded that life indoors has many compensations for which it is worth sacrificing some independence. Sir Isaac Newton (1643–1727) is rumoured to have invented the lockable cat door in an attempt to persuade his moggies to hunt for mice *inside* the house, instead of just those outside. We do not know whether this is true, or whether it were successful. Anyone familiar with cats, however, would suspect that they got the better of the bargain.

But if you are now suitably dressed and appropriately made-up, it is necessary to consider where to live while you pursue your Georgian adventure and how to earn some money.

Chapter Three

Home & Work

During the eighteenth century the rural population usually worked near or from their homes if they were agricultural workers, or skilled labourers such as weavers, blacksmiths, carpenters, stone masons and so forth. In towns and the few cities however, times were changing from the middle of the century as the Industrial Revolution gained traction. Entrepreneurs were wanting to use water and steam power to drive machinery, and develop mass production. Thomas Newcomen invented his 'atmospheric' engine in 1712 which condensed steam inside a cylinder, thus creating a vacuum and enabling the piston action to produce mechanical work. Hundreds of these engines were used in Britain and Europe, mostly to pump water out of mines, as growing industry needed coal; mines needed to expand down into lower levels without drowning everyone; and the fuel for the engine was on hand. However, with the difficulty of transporting coal and the basic inefficiency of the Newcomen engine, it was not the ideal solution for those entrepreneurs wanting a steam engine to expand their own, different and manufacturing, industrial activities.

In 1781, the Scotsman James Watt, realising that the Newcomen design wasted a great deal of the generated energy by repeatedly heating and cooling the cylinder, introduced his own version. This was very much more fuel-efficient, which made it both more productive and cheaper to run. The demand for the Watt engine and the necessity of accessing large quantities of fuel and raw materials, not to mention getting goods to market, led to the huge canal-building projects of the eighteenth century. Roads were rough, meandering, muddy, could only transport small quantities at a time ... and broke fragile products like valuable ceramics. Water was smooth, offered less resistance to the transportation of larger loads pulled by horses, and could be designed to take a more direct path given canal lock technology, unlike rivers. Between the 1770s and the 1830s, it is estimated that over 4,000 miles of canals were built, mostly in England. They connected the raw materials and fuel to the production sites, and then took the finished goods to market.

The most noted pioneer was the 3rd Duke of Bridgewater (1736–1803) who owned coal mines and wanted to get his fuel to the rapidly-industrialising town of Manchester. His business acumen and foresight, and the skill of his canal-builders, unleashed the only way to successfully solve the problems of the supply of fuel and raw materials, and satisfy market demand. Canal traffic was not exactly rapid in the eighteenth and early nineteenth centuries, of course, being horse-drawn. But it was much bigger in terms of loads, reciprocal business possibilities, and far less dodgy than the roads which were fraught with physical difficulties, and highwaymen.

There are many twenty-first century canal enthusiasts busy restoring forgotten stretches, so such a visitor to Georgian times might fancy building one from scratch with no mechanical assistance. It was back-breaking and often dangerous work, but paid better than farm labouring, and the provisions had to be sustaining. It has been reported that their diet was mostly beef and ale, and it is certainly true that the navvies eventually got a reputation for long and drunken binges when they went into towns and villages to let off steam after pay-day, whilst the general populace cowered behind closed doors.

If this does not appeal, but if the visitor still fancies an outdoor occupation filled with excitement, he could take to the roads and become a highwayman. Both the life-span and the reputation of the often-glamorised highwaymen, however, were becoming somewhat curtailed after the late eighteenth century, thanks to handguns and the Enclosure Act of 1773. The latter meant that stone walls severely hampered a get-away. Becoming an eighteenth century highwayman would not be easy for a modern mugger or thief since it would involve horse-riding skills, a disregard of the death penalty, and a willingness to lurk about in highly unpleasant and dangerous living conditions for, probably, little ultimate reward. Even if you managed to be a 'gentleman' highwayman, who was reputedly courteous to the victims he ambushed and robbed, you would probably end up on the gallows. This will be an early end to a dashing career, even if ordinary people do turn out to watch your brave demise and sympathetically cheer their folk hero. It is also probably worth mentioning here that eighteenth-century hangmen had mastered neither the positioning of the noose under the left ear, nor the concept of weight and drop for a rapid death due to a broken neck. Some of them, of course, must have given the matter considerable expert thought, but it was a public spectacle of deterrence, and so little consideration was given to the suffering of the strangled condemned.

Highwaymen were mostly quite young, and it was most often not a full-time job. A life of crime, thus, is probably not the best way forward for the time-traveller bent on finding somewhere to live and to 'earn' enough money to survive.

It would be much better for the visitor to capitalise unobtrusively on his or her present knowledge and skills. It would be advisable to take up residence in London, because the capital was the place in which intellectual ingenuity and 'property' returned the best rewards, such as invention, investment, banking, speculation, networking, politics, and the law. It has to be admitted that this is probably a career-path more suited to a man than a woman in the eighteenth century, but being a businesswoman was not impossible. Women were indeed active in business, although it tended to be in retail, taverns and brothels. But then, we girls have always known what people really want; shopping and sex, given that more elevated and intellectual occupations have traditionally been closed to us before modern times.

A fruitful arena of employment and income, however, might be natural philosophy, science or government. Even if you are not an accredited twenty-first century scientist, engineer or civil servant, you might still be able to earn a good living and reputation by dropping a few hints about hygiene, medicine, energy, astronomy, civil infrastructure, legal procedure, and verifiable accounting procedures – to name but a few. It might also be entirely possible through judicious networking to raise money for industrial projects. Such as developing the existing methods of filtering domestic water, experimenting with the combustibility and utility of coal gas, wondering about energy and gases in general, speculating about the structure of a theoretical Periodic Table – or just floating a new manufacturing company with an alluring 'new' product that guarantees profit, like an industrial loom. There should be no need for the enterprising visitor to worry about money, as a twenty-first century citizen who elects to spend time among the Georgians should be able to both improve their lot, and enrich his or hers.

In terms of inventions, the eighteenth century got off to a slow but steady and noteworthy start with Jethro Tull's seed drill, Cristofori's piano (rapidly succeeded by Shore's necessary tuning fork), and the Newcomen engine. The Georgians were considerably more polymathic than we are in our specialised times. Sir Edmund Halley (1656–1742) was an astronomer, physicist, geophysicist, meteorologist and mathematician. When not computing the orbit of his eponymous comet and being the Astronomer Royal, he also spent a lot of time under water and, in 1714, produced his own much-improved version of the diving bell, which was an ancient concept about which he had been thinking since 1691.

By the end of the eighteenth century it is quite startling to note the problem-solving capacity and sheer inquisitiveness of the Georgians and their European contemporaries. A roll-call of notable inventions includes the fire extinguisher, the mercury thermometer, the flying shuttle and the spinning jenny, the spinning frame and the spinning mule, the leyden jar (first electrical capacitator), the lightning rod, the English dictionary, the sextant, Harrison's Marine chronometer for determining longitude, the electric telegraph, the flushing toilet, the battery, the threshing machine, the safety lock, bifocal eyeglasses, the circular saw, the power loom, the gas turbine, gas lighting, the cotton gin and the carding machine, the preserving jar, and many more. A prototype steam boat was invented by John Fitch in 1786, and two brave souls also took a crack at the parachute and the submarine. Much of this inventiveness was driven either by the textile industries in England or the problems of navigation, both of which reflect the essentially expansionist cast of the Georgian mind.

Many of these inventions were prototypes or early patents, and it often took decades for a safe and efficient version to enter general use e.g. a steamship which did not blow up, or the distillation and distribution of coal gas. The many problems that needed to be overcome, however, would be an interesting and fertile source of occupation for any modern engineer or scientist time-traveller.

If, though, the visitor feels unequal to advancing the embryonic Industrial Revolution personally in an entrepreneurial, scientific or engineering capacity, there are many more ordinary jobs available in towns and cities. In London the economy was essentially pre-industrial, relied on manual labour, and businesses were small and generally employed only a few people. Those employees, moreover, would probably have got their jobs through either family or friend connections as employers often offered apprenticeships to each other's sons. This was a tradition which dates, in England, from the Middle Ages and probably reflects a weary parental acknowledgement that young teenagers are more effectively disciplined by just about anyone other than their own father and mother. Both boys and girls often followed their parents into the same place of employment, as taking on a total stranger was riskier from the employer's perspective. Despite this benevolent and practical attitude to recruitment, however, few people had secure jobs for life, and many had to work at more than one job to make ends meet.

Curiously, much of our knowledge of work is gleaned from criminal or civil records, such as the Old Bailey Proceedings, in which the occupations of both the victims and criminals are noted, and form a fascinating record of how erstwhile-employed men fell into a life of crime as the demand for their skills diminished. Indeed, the chaplain of Newgate prison in the Ordinary's Accounts notes the diverse and blameless jobs of many of his charges before they ended up so sadly. Other sources of information include coroner's inquest records, admissions to St Thomas's and other hospitals, and parish records.

Any time-travellers wanting to experience or improve the poorer citizens' lives in the eighteenth century will find that a nationwide culture of humanitarian relief is lamentably absent, which could be a problem for anyone wanting to help. People obviously were altruistic, but it was on a local and personal level, and very often affiliated to the church. Other sources of support for the disadvantaged were (some) landowners or well-off tenantry, and the parochial authority. The latter administered the existing Tudor Poor Laws on a local and somewhat haphazard basis, so a parish pauper could hope for a weekly pension of between a few pence and a few shillings, depending on where they lived. How well the poor were treated was thus what we would call a postcode lottery. It was not until the nineteenth century that the Poor Laws were revised to become a centralised system overseen by government and the law. This, however, did result in the widespread introduction of the dreaded institutionalised Workhouse, although local ones had existed before, and the Victorian notion of the 'deserving poor'.

Any visitor to Georgian times may be shocked by the apparent callousness of some of those who were in a position to help, but did not generally do so. However, one must appreciate that they did not understand mental illness, for example, and were both fearful of it and fascinated by it. Bedlam, as depicted by Hogarth in *The Rake's Progress*, was the oldest asylum, and it was a place of dreadful physical and mental abuse which was visited by the public for entertainment. Fear, in fact, was often responsible for any seeming lack of philanthropy in that the 'haves' have always been afraid of the 'have-nots'. The latter were often driven to crime, and the streets at night were dark and dangerous places; they spread diseases or, at least, diseases spread rapidly among them; they had no education, were poor workers, and drank. Certainly, in the eighteenth century, enlightened minds were discussing the fact that the problem of the poor was actually – poverty, but it would take longer for governmental recognition, and it would get worse as the Industrial Revolution progressed before it got better. It was the increasing influx of people into towns and cities in search of work from the mid-eighteenth century onwards, creating even worse social problems, that built even more fear and thus the eventual acceptance that something had to be done. The first guardians of the nation's social conscience and poor relief were therefore parish authorities and the church. Only well-off and locally respected men formed the parish council, of course, and the others had taken Holy Orders. This might seem rather a barrier to promoting modern social work ideas and solutions, but in fact parishes variously employed clerks, nurses, apothecaries, surgeons and watchmen. It is entirely possible that to be poor in the early eighteenth century was preferable to being poor 100 years' later, and that a twenty-first century humanitarian could find gainful paid employment. However, not many people in eighteenth-century England were employed in what we might regard as social or intellectual occupations.

Frankly, it is unlikely that a twenty-first century visitor could rival the eighteenth-century citizens when it comes to hard physical labour, or the artisan skills we have now largely lost. We do have one great advantage, however, and that is literacy, so we would make good clerks, government and legal employees, and bookkeepers. The disadvantage, of course, is that all records then were kept by hand, there being no typewriters, never mind keyboards. Those of us who now only ever hand-write a shopping list or occasionally scrawl our signature will find it arduous to say the least, especially using quill and ink. All books, news reports and articles were written by hand before being typeset for publication, but it would probably only take a few months to re-learn the basic art of speedy hand-writing, except that it was a formal art-form in commerce and government. Elegant calligraphic ability would tell potential employers a lot about your background, education, and status. Very few of us would pass muster. In fact, the progress towards modern and idiosyncratic bad handwriting is very evident among the hard-pressed officials charged with recording Census data, from the nineteenth century onwards. Some of it is barely legible. But that is in the future, and if a visitor can bring himself to endure life in a Georgian office, working long hours on a high stool among the ledgers, then this does have employment possibilities.

But what about women? A popular notion is that Georgian women presided regally over an organised domestic scenario, and that the poorer were doing the work. The rich, maybe, but not so much the aspiring middle classes, and certainly not the poor.

The advent in the eighteenth century of books about cookery and housekeeping suggests that domestic management and economy was a 'career' option in itself, although that will require a husband, house, and family. Even the most enthusiastic modern woman, wanting to experience a Georgian life, might balk at this prospect. It was, however, the destiny of most women of both reasonable or considerable means. We may think that, since they had servants, whether many or few, their life was cushioned from hands-on work. Servants, however, had to be managed, trained and monitored. Household accounts had to be scrupulously kept for both the husband's inspection, and as a guard against fraudulent deception by both staff and tradesmen.

A female job-seeker will find herself largely confined to domestic service if she wants to be in any way respectable. Women domestic servants earned less than men, of course. Wages for eighteenth-century women could range from £2 pa for the lowliest kitchen skivvies to between £6 and £8 for a housemaid, and up to £15 per annum for a skilled housekeeper. However, they usually did, at least, get lodging, food and probably a clothes allowance. They also had a considerable measure of personal security in an era when keeping a roof over one's head, and avoiding the dangers often associated with more 'independent' female occupations, were not to be so easily dismissed. For a young female servant in a wealthy household the greatest danger was either the predatory sons of the master, or the male servants. Pregnancy terminated all notions of respectability and employability, even in Georgian times – and they were more relaxed about this sort of thing than the Victorians.

There are many versions of the poem or song 'She was Poor but she was Honest.' Nobody even really knows the genesis of it, but it resonated from the nineteenth to the early twentieth century, and would have undoubtedly been understood in the eighteenth century. This version is almost certainly Victorian, and a music hall song:

> She was poor, but she was honest,
> Victim of the squire's whim:
> First he loved her, then he left her,
> And she lost her honest name.

Then she ran away to London,
For to hide her grief and shame;
There she met another squire,
And she lost her name again.

See her riding in her carriage,
In the Park and all so gay:
All the nibs and nobby persons
Come to pass the time of day.

See the little old-world village
Where her aged parents live,
Drinking champagne that she sends them;
But they never can forgive.

In the rich man's arms she flutters,
Like a bird with broken wing:
First he loved her, then he left her,
And she hasn't got a ring.

See him in the splendid mansion,
Entertaining with the best,
While the girl that he has ruined,
Entertains a sordid guest.

See him in the House of Commons,
Making laws to put down crime,
While the victim of his passions
Trails her way through mud and slime.

Standing on the bridge at midnight,
She says: 'Farewell, blighted Love.'
There's a scream, a splash--Good Heavens!
What is she a-doing of?

Then they drag her from the river,
Water from her clothes they wrang,

For they thought that she was drownded;
But the corpse got up and sang:

'It's the same the whole world over;
It's the poor that gets the blame,
It's the rich that gets the pleasure.
Ain't it all a bloomin' shame?'

Oh *dear*.

Our idea of domestic servants comes mostly from Victorian times. In the Georgian era, they did not usually wear uniforms or clothes denoting their work or rank in the household, except in the very grandest. No saucy maids' outfits, few fit young footmen clad in alluring and tight-fitting outfits, or butlers wearing formal clothes that aped their betters and lent them status. These were largely nineteenth century concepts. Most domestic jobs were physically very demanding, and the more desirable ones usually followed the Georgian principle of casual nepotism. The notion of equal opportunities among job applicants would have been considered absurd. However, the emerging role of the housekeeper might suit a modern woman, since aspiration among the better-off meant the delegation of as many managerial domestic responsibilities as possible. Other occupational possibilities for a single woman would include spinner, tailoress, milliner, midwife, milkmaid, or washerwoman.

A middle-class ambitious husband's career would inevitably have involved his wife in impressive hospitality, attendance at socially-influential events, religious affiliation, listening to politicians droning on, meeting the important, stashing away money, and joining the growing consumer culture to which he aspired. We would indeed call this networking and much of it, inevitably, devolved upon the wives. Busy men, happy in an exciting and externalised world, seemed blithely content to disregard the feelings and problems of their constrained women and to rely upon their spouses' domestic talents to smooth their own path to social success. One can understand this, as the eighteenth century was a man's world. But, given the capabilities of intelligent but domestically-constrained women, it was neither fair, nor indeed a role-model for national economic success since half the population were in supportive and not innovative capacities, whatever their abilities.

Some women have always fought back against a traditionally dutiful life, however. Among the inspirational role-models for modern women wanting to live and make a difference in European Georgian times are the astronomers Caroline Herschel and Maria Kirch; mathematicians and physicists Emilie du Chatelet and Maria Agnesi; and the Methodists Sarah Crosby, Anne Dutton, and Selina, Countess of Huntingdon. In Bologna, Laura Bassi was made professor of anatomy in 1732, and Anne Damer was a famous woman sculptor. Rather more belligerently, some women were noted for fighting and aggression. Both Mary Read and Anne Bonney were sentenced to death for piracy in the eighteenth century, although they both escaped the noose because they were allegedly pregnant. There are several records of girls joining up to fight in armies posing as young lads, for instance, Phoebe Hessel and Catherine Licken.

It would thus be entirely possible for a modern woman to make a difference in Georgian times, although she would probably have to be either rich, ferociously ambitious, strangely disconnected from normal society – or just heedless.

But whatever your choice of livelihood in the eighteenth century though, you will also need somewhere to live.

Most people rented properties, as the freeholds were held by the rich and aristocratic. The Duchy of Westminster, a vastly wealthy estate, began its plutocratic life as a seventeenth century marital land deal in London. Sir Thomas Grosvenor married one modestly-named Mary Davies who had inherited five hundred acres of swamp, orchards and pasture in Middlesex. It mostly lay as it was, until 1720 when the Grosvenors decided it had distinct potential, as London was expanding rapidly. They were right. It would eventually become Belgravia and Mayfair. The Grosvenor family became the fabulously-wealthy dukes of Westminster, but do they acknowledge Mary Davies? No, of course not, and not yet even now. This is strange.

The ultimate mastermind, however, was the swamp-drainer, property developer and brick-manufacturer, whom we instantly recognise – the early Victorian builder, Thomas Cubitt.

That finding somewhere to live, and negotiating the legal and financial work involved, was a matter of both concern and bewilderment is evidenced by a book written by the Rev. Dr John Trusler, the *London Adviser and Guide* (1786). To make matters clearer, he states

THE *London Adviser and Guide*: Containing every Instruction and Information Useful and Necessary to Persons Living in London and coming to reside there; In order to enable them to enjoy Security and Tranquility, and conduct their Domestic Affairs with Prudence and Economy* Together with an Abstract Of all those Laws which regard their protection against the Frauds, Impositions, Insults and Accidents to which they are there liable. Useful also to Foreigners.

Properties were let either furnished or unfurnished, as now, and as one would expect the further from the fashionable areas, the cheaper they were. The helpful Reverend is somewhat disdainful of lanes, courts, alleys, and such less appealing places. Susanna Ives, who interprets Trusler's book for the modern reader, tells us that

A private house 24 feet in front, and about seventy deep, two or three rooms on a floor, unfurnished, in the best streets, will let from 100 guineas a-year to 150; such a house, in other places, may be had from 80 to 100 guineas: unfurnished lodgings in such houses are seldom to be met with.

One hundred guineas in 1750 would have a twenty-first century value of about £9,000 which sounds a bargain, but since the average salary for a middle-class professional was only about £100 a year one can see that living in the best streets required a lot more than that. The First Lord of the Treasury, who we would now call the Prime Minister, earned £4,000 pa (about £350,000, which will bring tears to the eyes of our present leader who only earns about £140,000).

Would-be lessees are also warned about the hidden costs. Ground rent, levies (poor rates and land taxes), deposits for depreciation to furnishings and repairs, maintenance charges, and having to pay in advance etc. Not to mention the difficulties of sub-letting, or the problem of how much was the tenant's, and how much the landlord's, after a lengthy tenancy involving improvement to the property, or its fabric. Much of this we are entirely familiar with, but the Georgians evidently were less so, and could be lured into taking on more than they could financially cope with:

Fixtures removable are locks, bells, cisterns, grates, coppers, dressers, shelves, counters, &c. Paper pasted to the wall, buildings erected, new windows, chimney pieces, &c. or things to beautify the house, &c. and fixed to the freehold, must go with the house, at the end of the term, and cannot be removed.

In the eighteenth century, properties were already being sub-divided to maximise income to their landlords, with charges varying both with domestic amenities, and the ability to accommodate a servant. For the twenty-first century visitor, it seems likely that an unpleasant but cheap lodging might be the springboard for a life in the eighteenth century.

Before then, however, London was developing. The Georgian terraces that we now so cherish and which cost a small fortune were not generally built for the rich, but for the burgeoning middle classes. Maps from the seventeenth and eighteenth centuries show this expansion of the capital. Many of them degenerated into multiple-occupancy dwellings in late Victorian and Edwardian times before being gentrified for the wealthier after the 1870s, as the middle-classes were moving out to the fast-developing suburbs, aided by the railways. This exodus was not just driven by high rents in London and the developing transport system, but by the dreadful air quality in the city and the still ever-present sense of danger. The eighteenth century Dr Samuel Johnson wrote a poem, which he later fretted about. It does illustrate the social and political problems of being a Georgian Londoner, even if he did want to be one and retracted some of his thoughts in later, and more hopeful, times:

> Much could I add, — but see the boat at hand,
> The tide retiring, calls me from the land:
> Farewell! — When youth, and health, and fortune spent,
> Thou fly'st for refuge to the wilds of Kent;
> And tired like me with follies and with crimes,
> In angry numbers warn'st succeeding times;
> Then shall thy friend, nor thou refuse his aid,
> Still foe to vice, forsake his Cambrian shade;
> In virtue's cause once more exert his rage,
> Thy satire point, and animate thy page.

This is only partly understandable to the modern mind due to the neo-classical references including the 'Cambrian shade', which refers to Wales. However, the general idea about both the attractions and drawbacks of a London life still resonate, as we continue to wrestle with the problems of being both a rich and poor, vibrant, and multi-cultural city.

Settling in eighteenth-century London could still be fun and very interesting, though, whatever the difficulties. The Georgians, however, would most likely have pursued our more modern ideas when they could, whilst also trying to pay tribute to an older, and more religious, way of life. Being on the cusp of the Enlightenment, whilst also paying heed to more superstitious times, cannot have been easy.

Chapter Four

Health & Medicine

'Oh! Be thou blest with all that Heaven can send,
Long health, long youth, long pleasure – and a friend.'
Alexander Pope (1688–1744)

This is a somewhat wistful plea and one that, in the eighteenth century, was rather less likely to be fulfilled than now. Sharp-eyed readers will note that Alexander Pope died at the relatively early age of 56. This brings us to the subject of life expectancy in the eighteenth century and, in fact, for thousands of years before, given what we now know about the long-deceased from their bones and DNA.

The problem with life-expectancy statistics is that they generally predict longevity based at birth. So if historians tell us, for example, that most eighteenth-century people had a life expectancy of about forty years, one is inclined to assume that most people died at about forty, or thereabouts. This cannot possibly be true, of course. The fact is that if you survived your first year, your life expectancy rose brightly. If you survived your first five years, despite childhood viral illnesses and their bacteriological complications, it rose very considerably. If you survived until fifteen-years old, then you could possibly live to a ripe old age into your seventies or maybe eighties, even if you were later burdened by being a labourer on a rather basic diet and with a wearying lifestyle – or perhaps an idle and rich aristocrat incapacitated by an over-indulgent one.

Weighing the various explanations for these mortality reductions, the authors see three phases. From the mid-eighteenth century to the mid-nineteenth century, improved nutrition and economic growth played a large role, as did emerging public health measures. From the mid-nineteenth century to the early twentieth century, the delivery of clean water, removal of waste, and advice about personal health practices all led to lower mortality rates, though urbanization had the opposite effect, due to high mortality rates in cities. Since the 1930s, mortality reductions have been driven primarily by medicine, first by vaccination and antibiotics and later by the expensive and intensive interventions that characterize modern medicine.

We now have forensic anthropologists who can evaluate race, age, gender, diet and lifestyle, disease, and, often, cause of death from skeletal remains, and we do not only have archaeological evidence. We are the descendants of the survivors and, increasingly, we have genealogical and even genetic information about our forebears at our disposal, which was previously only the province of the aristocratic, who had family history and portraits upon which to draw. You may care to research who, among your forebears and relatives, did not survive to adulthood in an era before the mid-1800s or even the 1930s. This exercise may well be rather depressing, despite their inevitably large families.

Most of us today are the descendants of people who physically worked far harder than we ever have, and who paid for it in terms of health problems. So how did they fare, or even just cope, in the days before welfare and health services? And what will you do as a time-traveller, when ill-heath strikes – as it surely will – despite your feather-bedded immune system thanks to modern inoculations against viral diseases. What of your ability to withstand the bacterial effects of dirty water, rudimentary civic sanitation, ubiquitous parasites and domestic vermin, and no antibiotics?

For the poor, of course, inevitably deteriorating health was a financially desperate situation for both themselves personally, and their dependents. Not only did the adults have to worry about wounds, lockjaw, abscesses, childbirth and arthritis, but their infants were defenceless against dangerous diseases like scarlet fever, whooping cough, measles, and infant diarrhoea. There were few effective remedies available, save maybe from some religious or charitable establishments nearby which were, in the eighteenth century, trying to help, but usually unable to offer much other than herbal palliative care and prayer.

People in the eighteenth century thus placed considerable faith (or hope) in prayer, despite the fact that it was the Age of Enlightenment, possibly because the alternatives were limited. The commitment to rational science and a growing religious scepticism did not filter down to the masses for a very long while nor, indeed, result in effective treatments. Instead they had to depend largely upon God and their own resources, such as family remedies handed down, or a local 'wise woman' and her herbs. Many of our medicines are based on the pharmacology of plants and minerals, of course, but there is a difference between gulping down an extract of meadowsweet or willow bark and taking a regulated dose of synthesized aspirin. The Georgians were also well aware of the remedy of using cobwebs on wounds. This counter-intuitive treatment was used for thousands of years and it is now known that it worked because the webs are rich in vitamin K, which promotes blood clotting, and also possesses anti-fungal and anti-bacterial properties. It does though depend largely on the wound being thoroughly cleaned first with, for example, vinegar and honey – but we would much rather rely on antiseptics and a course of antibiotics.

Most people were unable to afford the services of a doctor, or were unwilling to involve them before it was absolutely necessary. Since the latter was often just as likely to kill the patient as cure him or her, many people were possibly better off without one. But even those who could afford a doctor sometimes seem to have first preferred a recourse to something rather less inevitably drastic, such as the home medicine chest (see below).

For those who could afford something, however, there was the growing profession of the apothecary or chymist, who generally charged less than the doctor, and who possibly offered less invasive and potentially lethal remedies. This was by no means certain, however, as there were few reliably accredited qualifications nor regulation of drugs and remedies. Until the early twentieth century, people could easily buy drugs and poisons which are now either illegal or prescription-only. Queen Victoria has often been accused of using drugs such as opiates (laudanum), cannabis and chloroform for various reasons, although this has never really been verified. If she did, however, it would hardly have been remarkable in her era as nearly everyone else did too, if they could. It is known that she received a hefty dose of chloroform during the birth of her fifth child, and thought it simply splendid. One can understand why, especially as she gave birth to nine children eventually. Other royal drug usage rumours, however, are largely unsubstantiated, although it is said that she smoked cannabis for pain medication. This has been dismissed on the grounds that she detested and forbade smoking, but that would only appear to have been indoors. During summer picnics on her beloved Balmoral estate she apparently discovered the efficacy of the cigarette in dispersing clouds of infuriating Scottish midges. This sounds like the sort of advice that her beloved ghillie and companion, John Brown, might have imparted as he settled Her Majesty on a tartan rug and unpacked the food and whisky for the two of them:

'Fer Gawd's sake, will ye just spark up, woman, afore we're eaten alive!'

'Pass the new safety matches then, Brown.'

The first line of defence against disease, for those who could afford it, was the medicine chest. In the eighteenth century, everyone very well knew that prevention was better than cure and, indeed, an option offering more likelihood of success. Middle-class households, therefore, often had a medicine chest and the duty of both protecting the healthy and administering to the sick fell upon the women. These women could not possibly have had any training but knew the burden of the health of their families fell upon their shoulders and, mainly, they only had family journals or books of remedies to help them. The precursor to a doctor's visit in the moderately well-off home, but especially for the traveller, was therefore the medicine chest.

The burgeoning Empire encouraged diplomats, soldiers, engineers, scientists, administrators, missionaries, educators and adventurers to travel great distances to destinations which were fraught with unfamiliar parasites and diseases, not to mention angry natives with aggressive intentions and weaponry. The journeys themselves were dangerous, never mind what one might encounter at the other end. Much of what is documented in the Georgian medicine chest is what we would now consider a placebo or a symptom-soother, rather than a cure. Explorers and early administrators of the Empire lived or died less from medical assistance than their own constitutions, or luck. Ships' surgeons had large medicine chests to cover the many eventualities arising from poor diet, infections, contagions and wounds, and the famous seventeenth and eighteenth century pirate captains also took the health of their crews very seriously. In fact, Blackbeard (Edward Teach d.1719) once ran out of medicines in Charleston Harbour and sent three of his most menacing crew members plus a hapless prisoner to the Governor of the Province, threatening to murder all the prisoners, send their heads to the governor and set fire to all the ships he had captured, unless the demanded medicine chest was forthcoming immediately. It was. Another pirate, Edward Low, made similarly bloodcurdling threats in Santa Cruz to seize a new medicine chest, which was also promptly despatched. These pirate captains had obviously not read the British Navy's advice to ships' surgeons to take twice the amount of medicine that they estimated might be necessary for the voyage. This advice might have been influenced by the example of HMS *Rainbow* in the late seventeenth century after the crew deserted on discovering that the medicine chest was empty. On board ships, the surgeons stocked up with many ingredients, scales and weights, and pestles and mortars, all packed in chests specially designed to maximise space, efficiency, and safety in rough seas. They were assisted by a number of manuals which included and succeeded the late seventeenth century publication on medicine at sea by John Woodall, the Surgeon-General to the East India Company.

Back on land, however, doctors were not generally supposed to mix and sell their own medicines as it was the preserve of the Worshipful Society of Apothecaries. This seems to have been a somewhat grey area, though, as in 1727 John Quincy MD published *The Dispensatory of the Royal College of Physicians* which is a pharmaceutical recipe book, written in English, and clearly targeted at anyone who was interested, whether doctor, apothecary or wife. Many of the ingredients sound pleasantly botanical, although that is certainly no guide to their safety, but inevitably one does come across references to even more doubtful or repulsive stuff like frog spawn, sulphur, white lead, urine, dung, and quick lime, as well as a considerable reliance on alcohol (as a preservative or suspension), and the one thing that certainly did work – opiates.

Domestic medicine chests, however, probably comprised ingredients bought from an apothecary, perhaps with a manual advising how to mix and use them in specific circumstances, such as *The Book of Phisick* (1710, anonymous).

A source of accessible help for the poorer masses often came from the barber-surgeon, particularly in the realm of dentistry, minor surgery and, of course, useless blood-letting (the reference source of the barber's red and white pole outside the shop). A sober and steady hand, essential for barbering with a cut-throat razor, must have assisted their experience and expertise. Since apprenticeships usually began in the early teens, a man could be qualified and free to practise his skill from the age of about twenty-one, and this system dated from the Middle Ages. The ubiquitous practice of blood-letting (phlebotomy) has a very long history indeed and seems to arise in many different classical theories of disease and treatment, but it usually related to ideas about the 'humours' of the body being out of balance, or 'under tension' due to too much blood or heat. These are vague concepts and therefore somewhat resistant to proof as to whether they ever did any good or not. By the late-eighteenth century some experienced and more scientifically-minded doctors were wondering aloud whether bleeding a patient did not actually weaken them, sometimes fatally, but in less exalted circles the practice persisted into the nineteenth century. The Church actually forbade those stand-in doctors, the monks and priests, from practicing blood-letting as it was 'abhorrent', albeit only for religious reasons. Blood-letting could be achieved from arm or neck by surgical instruments, or 'naturally' – with leeches. Leeches, of course, had to be collected from the wild or specially bred and raised which was hardly easy, and even before the eighteenth century medical practitioners of all sorts had realised that the wriggly creatures laboriously harvested from ponds and ditches were likely to be rather dirty. Most phlebotomies, thus, were carried out using a blade (the fleam) and bowls or, by Georgian times, with the technological artificial leech or scarificator. This was a very uninviting object which punched a circle of horizontal cuts into a vein, rather like a real leech does, and often had a syringe attached with which to draw the blood. It was more precise and less agonising than someone slashing at the arm or neck with a single blade and then forcing blood out into a bowl. Many patients, however, might have preferred the real leeches as they, at least, had the decency to inject an anaesthetic first, if only to ensure that you didn't know they were latching on to you.

Time, knowledge, and science have moved on however, if rather slowly before the late nineteenth century. But what goes around comes around and twenty-first century science has discovered a use for both the (sterile) leech in microsurgery and a benefit of blood-letting, although only for a very few specific and rather rare conditions.

During the seventeenth and eighteenth centuries the authorities became aware of the very random nature of medical knowledge scattered around among 'society' doctors, apothecaries, barber-surgeons, wise women, and mere charlatans, and decided that perhaps something should be done to harness and regulate it. The Worshipful Company of Apothecaries was established in 1617, largely to separate them from the Grocers' Guild and to challenge the College of Physicians' monopoly on the right to practise medicine. In 1704 members gained the legal right to practise medicine and, in 1815, were given the right to license and regulate medical practitioners throughout England and Wales. Membership, however, nearly always depended upon experience (apprenticeships) and recommendation, and not formal training in medical schools and written examinations. Since the Colleges of Physicians and

Surgeons were more interested in treating the wealthy, the more egalitarian Worshipful Company could be regarded as the forerunners of the GP. It would be easy now to dismiss the colleges' choice of wealthier patients as snobbish or financially motivated, but in fact nearly all medical practitioners were necessarily interested in two things; efficacy and results. The richer the patients, the more income the practitioner had to spend on science, research and his own reputation. The poorer the patients, and the more experience one had in trying to help them, the greater the contribution to the health and well-being of the workers, who ultimately became ever more important as the Industrial Revolution progressed. The two approaches eventually converged, especially in the nineteenth century when thousands turned to industry for employment and swelled the urban populations, and brought with them additional problems of over-crowding, injury and disease.

One of the medical giants of the eighteenth century was John Hunter (1728–1793), regarded as the Father of Surgery, and now celebrated in the Hunterian Museum at the Royal College of Surgeons in London which houses those of his estimated 14,000 specimens that remain. He made money from the rich, including George III, but spent much of it on the research that was his real passion, being an early advocate of practical observation and scientific method. A visit to the Hunterian Museum will convince you that the man spent both years and money in the pursuit of anatomical knowledge. Few things in the animal or plant kingdoms upon which he could lay his hands and employ his dissecting instruments escaped his curiosity, when not attending to the royal family. He revealed, made copious notes and drawings, pickled, taught, and wrote textbooks. He also experimented surgically on people, for whom we should feel great sympathy and whose courage born of necessity we should salute, since we have been the beneficiaries. Hunter's background was the perfect storm for such an eminent career. He began his career as an anatomist at his elder brother, William's, anatomy school. He then spent time as an army surgeon, which was always a formative experience under the worst of circumstances, and then worked with a dentist, James Spence, whose abiding interest was tooth transplants (innovative, grisly … and sometimes, but not always, unsuccessful).

Hunter is credited with contributing greatly to the understanding of the separate blood circulations of foetus and mother, child development, venereal diseases, bone growth, teeth, gunshot wounds and inflammation, and the lymphatic system. He also pioneered many surgical procedures such as the tracheotomy. During his career a number of the great London hospitals were established which made the dissemination of medical knowledge much easier, and encouraged research. Guy's Hospital was founded in 1724, St George's in 1733, and the Middlesex in 1745.

But there were so many ways to die in the eighteenth century that it is surprising how many people lived long enough to develop the tough immune systems they must have had to survive. Before embarking on your Georgian adventure, therefore, you would be well advised to ensure that your tetanus jab is up to date, together with cholera, influenza, and pneumonia vaccinations. You might think it a pity that, since its global eradication, it is no longer possible to have a smallpox inoculation since this was a horribly familiar, and most feared, disease. Edward Jenner (1748–1823) is usually credited with being the man who discovered how to inoculate people against this scourge. He did it by using a live cow-pox serum which he obtained from an infected milk-maid, having correctly observed that milk-maids did not get smallpox if they had previously had cowpox, which many of them had. He then 'inoculated' an 8-year-old boy named James Phipps, the son of his gardener, with the pus from a cowpox sufferer, and then deliberately infected him with smallpox. The child survived unscathed, which subsequently saved millions of lives over the decades. This is so often the case. We know, of course, that this would never get past a research ethics committee today in a democracy. Nor, indeed, would most of the experiments in the past, upon the insights of which we have so depended for our medical progress and health. People and animals have suffered and died that we might not.

However, Edward Jenner was not the first person to discover the benefits of smallpox inoculation. He was not even the first person to notice that cowpox sufferers were immune to smallpox. Others to have made the connection included a physician named John Fewster and a Dorset farmer named Benjamin Jesty who successfully 'inoculated' his family with cowpox during a local smallpox epidemic. Jenner, however, was the scientist who assembled and documented the proof and brought it to the attention of the medical profession, being a Member of the Royal Society. Prior to that some intrepid souls had made the rather riskier connection between infecting someone from a source of mild smallpox and the unlikelihood of their later contracting a fatal or disfiguring form of it, which was called variolation.

Lady Mary Montagu Wortley (1689–1762) was an unusual and very feisty woman, and a keen pioneer of what we would call women's rights, although she was mainly concerned with asserting the equality of women's intellectual abilities rather than political power. She was also an intrepid traveller with her ambassador husband and family, and fascinated to learn about the lives of women outside England. On her husband's appointment as Ambassador to Turkey she discovered the local procedure of inducing immunity to smallpox while visiting *zenanas* (harems) and befriending the women in them, and lost no time in protecting her own children against it. Her brother had died in 1713 from smallpox and she herself was slightly scarred from the effects of the disease, which she had contracted two years later. The procedure she witnessed in Turkey was variolation, which involved introducing the pus from a mild case of smallpox into the bloodstream of a healthy child via a scratch. It does not sound very pleasant, but it did work. She became a very enthusiastic promoter of the procedure once back in England but the medical establishment was not keen, largely because it was an Oriental idea and thus not to be trusted. Jenner's later cowpox inoculation was, it must be admitted, much safer.

Despite the fact that you could possibly guard against smallpox if you are prepared to knock on Lady Mary's door and look the other way as the 'mild' smallpox pus is scratched into your arm, I would be tempted to smuggle along a few courses of wide-spectrum antibiotics, painkillers, steroids to reduce inflammation, and very definitely any preparations that kill head lice, fleas, ticks and tapeworms. Even a remedy designed for big dogs might seem attractive because you will be vulnerable to parasitic infections and be repelled by them, not having a Georgian stoic acceptance that life is just like that. But let us examine what is likely to happen when, and not if, you fall ill.

Firstly, this will not be unusual. Your family, friends, landlord or landlady, and fellow lodgers, will take your illness very much for granted since nearly everyone over the age of forty will be afflicted in some way or another, and not a few long before. By that age nearly everyone will be suffering dental and enteric problems caused by diet and contaminated food and water, and the potentially fatal effects of these should not be underestimated. Babies died from desperate diarrhoea episodes and the Georgians, as had so many others before them, certainly knew how lethal a tooth abscess could be, and that the only solution was unhygienic draining or painful extraction. Any sort of uncontrollable sepsis (blood-poisoning), from either wounds or abscesses, was often a one-way ticket to the grave.

Dr Samuel Johnson (1709–1784) suffered from very poor health all his life and his diagnosed ailments included scrofula, gout, a stroke, and persistent depression, which was accompanied by panic attacks, breathlessness, and a fear of insanity. His friends were alarmed by this litany of misfortune and did their best to help him even, sometimes, taking him into their own homes to nurse him. Unknown at the time was the condition of Tourette's Syndrome with its involuntary tics, sudden inappropriate vocalisations, odd gestures, and obsessive-compulsive rituals. All of these were regularly observed in Johnson and which embarrassed, worried and bewildered his friends, but they always continued to support him. He was fortunate in that he was not poor even if not very rich, and he had an intellectual reputation, and social and political connections.

Those engaged in hard manual labour will be beginning to feel the effects of arthritis and any previous accidents, like broken limbs, from which they hoped they had recovered successfully. Poorer people living in damp and mouldy accommodation will be smitten by lung diseases and allergies, parasites, and the consequences of dangerous hygiene. Nobody knew about germs, but they did recognise the danger of airborne transmission of infection, although they could not explain it. They sensed that bad smells could contaminate an otherwise healthy environment, but did not understand the relationship between a ghastly odour and basic hygiene, and consequent infection. They noticed the symptom, but did not understand the causality. The other main environmental culprit was the 'miasma', which was an odourless gas which caused illness, they thought. This was quite an enduring belief since it was impossible to prove it either way.

As usual with the progress of human affairs, the clues abounded long before the principles of germ theory and contagion were finally established in science in the nineteenth century. Galen, the 2nd Century Greek physician proposed the enduring miasma theory, but others had different ideas after that, using the new technology of optics to see tiny things invisible to the naked eye. One Girolamo Fracastoro, as early as 1546, presciently suggested that disease was caused by 'seed-like' entities which could transmit infection with or without contact, and over distances. The seventeenth-century Italian, Francesco Redi, proved that bad things did not just generate spontaneously with some ingenious experiments with flies, their eggs and maggots, and decomposing organic material. As early as 1656, one Athanasius Kircher observed micro-organisms under his early microscope which led him to a 'germ' theory of the plague.

However, even in the seventeenth and early eighteenth century, doctors had little access to cutting-edge research or the brilliant but isolated insights of earlier times. They preferred to follow their training and still vaguely believe in the four Greek Hippocratic humours, (blood, phlegm, yellow bile and black bile) or at any rate a theory of 'balance', the miasma, and the benefits of bleeding or purging their long-suffering and, possibly terminally ill, patients. Interestingly, one class of medical victim which suffered particularly from the attentions of their physicians was royalty. They nearly all had more than one (quarrelling) doctor in attendance around the sickbed, and the stakes were inevitably high. Poor Charles II, the seventeenth century 'Merry Monarch', had a particularly despondent death at the hands of his frantic physicians who bled, purged, starved, cupped and burned, and induced vomiting in the unfortunate king for four tortuous days. They could not allow him to die peacefully. His last words to his courtiers are reported to have been 'I am sorry, gentlemen, for being such a time a-dying.' It is unclear whether he was apologising for inconvenience to them, or merely saying how he personally felt about the whole ghastly business. It is alleged that he converted to Catholicism on his deathbed although the veracity of this claim continues to be disputed. However, as the father of a reputed twelve illegitimate children a deathbed conversion, confession and absolution might have appealed to him, and his last thoughts were about his two most beloved mistresses, Nell Gwyn and Louise de Kerouaille, and not his barren and long-suffering wife, Catherine of Braganza.

Protestant Queen Anne, married to George of Denmark but reigning alone and in her own right, endured an alleged eighteen pregnancies which resulted in miscarriages, still-births, and infant deaths. She had one son who survived infancy, William the Duke of Gloucester, but who still only lived until the age of eleven. She was the queen, but that her main role was to produce a viable and, preferably, male heir was profoundly evident. It is also rumoured that she enjoyed a lesbian relationship with Sarah Churchill, the Duchess of Marlborough – and no wonder, if it is true. It would have been much safer and, possibly, more fun. It was the failure of Queen Anne to bear a surviving heir, of course, that led to the Elector of Hanover, George Ludwig, a Protestant cousin, becoming King George I. He was descended from James I via his mother, Sophia, and grandmother, Elizabeth of Bohemia. For Robert

Walpole, his chief minister, this linguistic handicap must have proved a boon as it inevitably led to greater authority for Parliament and the beginnings of a constitution with even fewer monarchical powers. George Ludwig neither understood the English language well nor really cared very much, and was homesick.

Georgian kings suffered slightly less than their forebears from the dubious attentions of their physicians as a rule, although poor 'mad' King George III certainly went through the medical mill. George I and George II had acute episodes relating, probably, to strokes which luckily killed them before their doctors could get into their professional stride. George I collapsed in his carriage on his way to Osnabruck in Germany and George II allegedly keeled over on the lavatory in England; both were either in a coma or dead before the doctors could try their best, or do their worst, to revive them. George III is now generally suspected to have suffered from porphyria rather than madness, particularly since he recovered. His main doctor was Francis Willis who specialised in treating the insane. His royal patient underwent the usual remedies such as coercion, restraints, strait jacket, blistering and fasting but, despite this, Willis reputedly showed much more kindness and consideration to all his patients than most of his fellow 'mad' doctors. In the eighteenth century, mental illness was generally regarded as evidence that the sufferer was sub-human. Even then, however, some enlightened and compassionate souls, like Willis, disagreed.

Women, of course, had an additional danger to survive, not just once but, usually, many times. They suffered from childbirth complications such as prolapses, dreadful fistulas or puerperal fever (sepsis), to such an extent that it was usual for any woman of financial means to make a will before her due date. Pregnancy and childbirth must have been both thrilling and terrifying – and inevitable. All our female forebears obviously managed to bring our ancestors into the world, of course, but some would have died by their late thirties or early forties, struggling to give birth to either a last stillborn or a maternal orphan. Men, however, no matter if personally bereaved by the loss of a loved wife, usually regarded this as a normal, if painful, course of events. We may suspect men of being less caring of their spouses in the eighteenth century, but there is plenty of evidence of their sorrow, even if they did remarry with what we might regard as indecent haste, and often for purely practical reasons. Working fathers needed a step-mother to care for the many children they were trying to raise, and many less-than-beautiful or impecunious single women were grateful for the opportunity to leave their parental homes, in which they were sometimes little more than servants, and take a chance on a life elsewhere with a widower and their own household.

Although many people were still relying on folk remedies of varying degrees of efficacy and prayer, those in the cities and, particularly London, were already being seduced by media advertising for patent medicines. The Victorian era was, of course, the great age of fantastic medicinal claims which promised to cure everything from warts to cancers. There was little regulation of medical practice and none at all of advertising, so snake-oil salesmen could lure the gullible, hypochondriac or desperate into trying just about anything. This money-making bonanza began in the eighteenth century with the journals themselves promoting the practice of advertising in editorial puffery:

> I look upon them as pieces of domestic intelligence, much more interesting than those paragraphs which our daily historians generally give us, under the title of home news ... the advertisements are filled with matters of great importance, both the great, vulgar, and the small.
>
> *Fog's Weekly Journal* (1736)

In fact, most advertisements were disguised as news items, which we would now call advertorials, especially as accompanying graphics were comparatively rare in newspapers and magazines. Canny copy-writers well knew the ways to engage the reader's attention, with appeals to desperation and snobbery being foremost. If a manufacturer could claim any sort of royal patronage this, of course, was excellent, but in fact any sort of aristocratic connection would suffice. Failing this, vague claims such as 'a lady of distinction' might do the trick, as in an advertisement of 1806 for Prince's Cherry Lotion (at half a guinea a bottle, so not cheap) which allegedly firmly re-anchored the lady's loose teeth to her great satisfaction – although not before she had already lost a couple due to being ignorant of this amazing elixir. The advertisers had already recognised the profit potential of the prophylactic use of their useless product, as well as for a 'cure'.

Dentistry has never been pleasant, but it has always been necessary. As everyone has always known, even before the advent of processed sugar, tooth abscesses were potentially lethal and had to be drained. The fact that they were located in the head, and in close proximity to the brain, throat, and glands made them dangerous indeed. And painful to resolve.

Georgian dentistry was only for the redoubtable or desperate, and very often involved charlatan tooth-pullers at fairs and markets, while those onlookers who did not happen to have toothache watched fascinatedly and, probably, nervously.

Thomas Berdmore, who was George III's 'Operator for the Teeth' wrote a definitive textbook on all matters dental in 1770. It is, however, probable that Berdmore knew about, and had read, a treatise on dentistry written by an extraordinarily prescient and long-lived man called Pierre Fauchard (1678–1761). Berdmore would have had to have read it in either French or German, however, as the first English translation was not published until 1946 by which time it was of mainly, if considerable, historical value. Monsieur Fauchard was a French physician who became very interested indeed in teeth and is known as the Father of Modern Dentistry. He is remarkable because he actually shared his knowledge and experience, which was somewhat unusual for the secretive eighteenth century as the most talented medical practitioners used to jealously guard their knowledge and skills. He published his seminal work in 1728, which began to raise dentistry to the level of a profession and, somewhat unsurprisingly, his ideas and expertise were keenly embraced by that home of the gleaming and perfect smile, the USA.

Pierre's innovative knowledge and experience embraced both fundamental, and embryonic cosmetic, dentistry. In Georgian times training began young, and when 15-years old he joined the French navy to become a surgeon. His tutor, Surgeon-Major Poteleret, was particularly interested in oral diseases, and since sailors were prone to both scurvy and oral damage, as well as caries and abscesses, it proved a training ground of wide variety. Fauchard left the navy and set up practice in Angers in 1700 at the age of only 22, but seven years of doubtless grim naval experience had left him very much more trained, competent and scientific than his contemporary practitioners, none of whom had any formal training, and all of whom were unregulated. In 1719 he moved to Paris. His two-volume treatise, which ran to over 800 pages, was a model of thoroughness and expertise and discussed and illustrated all aspects of dentistry: oral surgery, orthodontics, periodontics, false teeth, as well as the underlying sciences of anatomy, pathology and pharmacology. One rather wonders to whom he entrusted the care of his own teeth; he must have been a somewhat daunting patient,

'Monsieur Fauchard vient demain à 10h00 pour un check-up.'

'Oh, mon Dieu!'

Fauchard designed and had made his own dental instruments, and rather worrying they look now, although not altogether unfamiliar; the Elizabethans had far worse.

The development of cosmetically-pleasing and efficient false teeth was of considerable interest in the eighteenth century, both in Europe and America, and the time-traveller may well find himself staring in fascinated horror at some of the grim results in the mouths of the better-off. George Washington (1732–1799) is well-known to have been a martyr to his dreadful teeth although his dentures, contrary to persistent rumour, were not made of wood. They were, apparently at various times, made from ivory, hippopotamus or walrus teeth, and set into a lead base, which hardly sounds either comfortable or wise. They looked terrible, did not work, and were usually removed for eating. At least, however, he did not commission dentures made from human teeth from corpses or slaves, as others notoriously did. The fact, though, that we know so much more about the dental problems of the Founding Fathers than we do about those of Georgian monarchs is a testament to the American obsession with dental health. Only Thomas Jefferson, among the Founding Fathers, had a handsome and trouble-free mouth, which was much admired and commented upon.

So much for teeth. However, in addition to those vaccinations, the time-traveller might consider it judicious to have a thorough dental check-up before risking the attentions of an English eighteenth-century dentist who, unless you could afford Mr Berdmore, would have almost certainly not have been as skilled as Pierre Fauchard. Even then, it would be a dire prospect indeed for those many of us who shrink from the fleeting pain of the modern anaesthetic needle even after the gum has been numbed.

Whilst on the subject of self-inflicted lifestyle horrors, grave consideration must be given to what the Georgians usually referred to as the pox, or what we call sexually-transmitted diseases. Eighteenth-century sufferers felt considerable shame and fear when confronted with the ghastly evidence and were reluctant to seek treatment, and anyway their doctors found it difficult to distinguish between gonorrhoea and syphilis or, indeed, completely different complaints, such as scurvy. Cities, especially ports, were hotspots for venereal infection and the diseases spread in a commendably egalitarian way, from sailors and their doxies to the highest echelons of society, but often also sadly afflicting the innocent such as faithful wives and their unborn infants.

It is entirely probable that the twenty-first century time-traveller would initially be reluctant, to say the least, to have 'congress' with an eighteenth century citizen due to personal hygiene issues, lice and bed-bugs ... but habituation may eventually reduce both reluctance and resolve. To preserve your health, you should perhaps consider the symptoms and the treatments available before succumbing to the siren call of sexual companionship, wherever found. In men, the symptoms were usually rather more obvious than in women and it is probable that the latter were underdiagnosed. Besides the vaguer nature of the signs of venereal infection, a woman was more likely to face other distressing consequences; if she herself were virtuous then only her husband could be the culprit, and if she were not virtuous then the prospect of a horrifying chain of social opprobrium loomed. The men, however, would be left in little doubt that something was dreadfully wrong, since they might ultimately be leaking foully from almost every orifice, suffering ulcerated skin, swollen testicles and impotence, or even facing the eroded nose along with the madness and death of final-stage syphilis. They might well hope that their problems were due to a different, and more innocent, disease. Doctors themselves were inclined to find the clear evidence of a licentious lifestyle hard to believe in some evidently respectable patients. In 1721 the physician, Thomas Hewitt, when faced with a 60-year-old man presenting with ulcerated skin, lethargy and pain, and some truly appalling rectal problems, struggled to find a different diagnosis from the one staring him in the face, on the grounds that his patient was 'an honest trustworthy gentleman.'

The diagnosis did not really help, though, since there were no cures until the early twentieth century. The tendency of eighteenth-century doctors was to fight fire with fire, so to speak, so they dosed their unfortunate patients with compounds of sulphur, arsenic or mercury, all of which caused even more trouble and distress, not to mention being potentially fatal. They also experimented with various surgical procedures which must have been as agonizing as they were useless.

However, not everything medical in Georgian times was still proving as opaque to the scientific progress of the early modern era.

If you inadvertently leave behind your spectacles in the twenty-first century, then you need not worry too much, especially if you are long-sighted. By the eighteenth century, nearly every middle-class person had access to reading glasses (magnifiers). Even Henry VIII, in the sixteenth century, had a rudimentary pair perched on his nose to help him squint suspiciously at the written advice of his advisors and underlings as he grew older, and he was by no means the first. Assisting vision goes back as far as thirteenth-century Italy with the first eyeglasses being made in the late 1200s, and contemporary writers remarked on how rapid the development and adoption of glasses was. Early glasses only had convex lenses to help with long-sightedness, and it was not until the seventeenth century that Johannes Kepler published his treatise on how and why convex and concave eyeglasses remedied both long and short sight. Benjamin Franklin (1706–1790), the renowned American Founding Father and polymath, found himself suffering from both his usual short sight and age-related long sight (presbyopia) in later years and immediately set about inventing the bifocal, not being the sort of man to put up with a problem if he could do something about it, although he did not manage to salvage his teeth.

Older women, who were often charged with the duty of sewing clothes and fine embroidery, certainly suffered from presbyopia and could hardly be expected to undertake such meticulous work without ocular assistance. It is rather unlikely that anyone really considered the problems of the ageing ladies unless they held some financial power, but their usefulness was certainly important. If one were one of the lucky ones to live into old age, then one would want to continue to be useful, whether it was sewing or just minding the grandchildren. Indeed, the earliest example of magnifying spectacles, dating to circa 1400, were found in a nunnery in Germany, most likely to assist in the reading of religious tracts.

By the eighteenth century the practice of optics was rather more advanced than that of dentistry. It was, of course, less invasive and not terrifying at all in terms of treatment although, oddly, the adoption of spectacles which followed the contours of the head and curved behind the ears was rather slow. It was more usual for them to grip the nose. The lorgnette was popular in Georgian times, but it at least had the advantage of allowing the user to raise it imperiously and glare balefully and intimidatingly at others.

The Georgians were fighting a dispiriting if familiar battle against disease and ageing but, it has to be said, they were beginning to win with their advantages of increasing economic wealth, the Enlightenment culture of science and rationality, and the growing tendency of government to intervene to protect society from its worst excesses and mistakes. Medics were writing and sharing knowledge, and the new hospitals with their training ethic facilitated this; philosophers and scientists were questioning centuries-old assumptions about knowledge and reality; and advances in technology made it seem, perhaps, achievable during their lifetimes, at least in the rarified gathering-places of the intelligentsia; the masses would have to wait rather longer for effective remedies and relief, of course.

But before anyone is tempted to assume that it was only the suffering of the people that has driven the establishment of our public health care because of both the economic consequences of industrialisation and a developing social conscience, then spare some time to read the truly shocking account of the mastectomy endured by breast-cancer sufferer Fanny Burney, without anaesthetic, in 1811. She demonstrated astounding courage, survived, and wrote about it unflinchingly and without self-pity.

Although they might seem gullible to us, one must view the willingness of the Georgians to believe in fantastical medical claims in the context of their times, which were both more hazardous and haphazard than ours. In any case, we are hardly much more rational ourselves when it comes to buying over-the-counter remedies.

Branding was in its relative infancy in the eighteenth century, although becoming rapidly and firmly established, and it offered the consumer what he or she most wanted – reassurance. We are little different, with most of us paying four times as much for a branded pain-killer than its identical generic, but unbranded, counterpart. If our laws still allowed us to buy medicinal preparations containing opiates, belladonna, arsenic, strychnine, cannabis and alcohol – we undoubtedly would. Such ingredients, even if doing nothing whatsoever to address the cause of a disease, most probably made the sufferer feel (woozily) much better, in the short term, at least. It is easy now to feel more virtuous and sophisticated, but it is often not rational.

One of the most famous quack Georgian advertisements was for the 'Anodyne Necklace'. Oddly, the clue to the inefficacy of this thing was in its name, as 'anodyne' means bland, neutral, or unremarkable, which is hardly much of a recommendation in a patent medical cure. However, it sounded good, and all you had to do was hang it around the neck, which must have been a considerable attraction when you consider the alternatives on offer from your local medical practitioner armed, as he was, with his blood-letting and purging equipment. Not to mention his fees, and the consequent imputations of his superiority, which grew with his reputation and diminished the ability of the ignorant and afflicted to ask pertinent questions. Some eighteenth-century doctors obviously do have a brilliant and scientific track-record leading directly to our era, but far more do not.

The etymology of the word 'quack' has a long history, pre-dating the eighteenth century, which suggests that people were well aware that they were vulnerable to medical ignorance and incompetence, cynical fraud, and their own fears and hopes. The term was originally attached to the itinerant rogues who travelled the country, visiting markets and fairs, hoping to defraud the ignorant and desperate. The University of Michigan (Ann Arbour) has a website on which you can post your medical symptoms on a message board and find out what an eighteenth-century English or American quack might have prescribed. It is not very encouraging but it is, however, rather interesting.

As a twenty-first century time-traveller, you will probably find it kinder not to challenge the Georgians' hopes and beliefs unless you can offer an alternative, and effective, practical solution. Like, maybe, just thoroughly washing hands with hot water and soap, both of which the well-off, and the doctors, did have available to them – even if they mostly failed to do so. But you know about bacteria and viruses; they didn't. They did, however, pay whatever considerable attention they could to health ... and fitness.

Chapter Five

Fitness & Sport

'If we could give every individual the right amount of nourishment and exercise, not too little and not too much, we would have found the safest way to health.'

Hippocrates (c. BC 400)

What if you were young, fit and attractive? How to keep that way, as wished for by Alexander Pope, and to benefit from health, youth, pleasure, and a friend? The wealthier Georgians, or the men at least, were rather interested in health and fitness.

The classical Greek civilisations laid equal importance upon the fitness of both young men and girls, if largely to support either war or to promote the birth of healthy children, as indeed did the Romans. The ruling elders, quaffing their wine and probably abandoning fitness for politics and philosophy as they aged, encouraged calisthenics and games among the young. Gymnastics have not changed much for millennia, although our versions are somewhat safer. We may somersault over vaulting horses, but a fresco of Minoan art at Knossos (c. BC 1450) shows both sexes doing it for real over the horns of a charging bull (instructions diagram helpfully added later).

The ladies probably would have been keen too, but had no real opportunities to build their core strength, hone their muscles to perfection, run around in garments offering physical freedom, and resoundingly smack an impertinent beau in the face. Some powerful and well-bred ladies might have been intellectually intimidating (and usually regarded as too clever by half), but few were physically, hampered as they were by their clothes, social diktats, and family conventions. Among the less restrained lower orders, however, there were some very physically-formidable women. (Gallus Mag was a six-foot female bouncer in the early nineteenth century at a bar called The Hole in the Wall who reputedly had a jar of ears which she had bitten off misbehaving customers; happily for the British, this was in New York).

When it comes to the organised sporting fitness of the wealthier, however, we sadly have to exclude half the population (women) whose only recourse was walking, dancing or riding. That said, of course, they probably got far more exercise than we generally do.

One fitness solution was swimming. We all teach our children to swim as a matter of course today, but in the eighteenth century it was a rather unusual accomplishment – except among the wealthier. Most sailors could not swim which must have been rather alarming for them, given their work. When Admiral Sir Cloudesley Shovell's ship, HMS *Association*, ran aground off the shores of the Scilly Isles in 1707, over 800 sailors drowned, despite being quite close to land. The toll rose to over 2,000 as other ships in the flotilla also succumbed to the rocks. It is probable that few would have been saved by the rather heartless and opportunistic denizens of the Scilly Isles who were mainly interested in looting these apparently rich strangers, but it is equally probable that if more of them had known how to swim, they might have saved themselves.

Captain James Cook was murdered on a Hawaiian beach in 1779 while some of his men anxiously hovered offshore in a longboat, hoping to rescue him if he would only dash into the waves. None of them could swim, however, although this might not have saved him as his Polynesian assailants certainly could. Learning to swim proficiently off a balmy Pacific island was rather different, of course, than taking to the grey and chilly British waters.

Georgian gentlemen, however, were interested in this skill. Not only did it promote physical health, but it was also fun and competitive. The problem was where, and how, to do it, especially when urban rivers were hardly inviting. Nobody except poor urchins would have been very keen to swim in that open sewer, the Thames, or its local tributaries, like the Fleet, the Tyburn, the Westbrook, or Counters Creek. Even if one had known nothing about germ theory, the general stench surrounding inner London's waterways would have been distinctly off-putting, since they were usually conduits for sewage and highly-polluting industrial activity, like tanning. The toll of disgusting effluvia and dead dogs and cats rolling to the Thames via the Fleet are well documented and, in 1846, it actually exploded due to a build-up of decomposition gases which subsequently led to it being entombed underground by the aghast authorities, and ultimately becoming the sewer it is today.

There are, today, about twenty rivers, north and south, buried beneath our capital in sewers and culverts. It is possible to track their paths by following the dips and rises in modern roads, and some of their (now) feeble outpourings into the Thames can be seen at times of rain or flood. In Georgian times, the upper reaches of these tributaries were vigorous and considerably less contaminated than they would later become in Victorian times after the city expanded but, even so, they were not very convenient for the inner-city dweller given that the only mode of transport was walking or riding. One example of Georgian health-giving waters was Bagnigge Wells, which was situated in our present and very urban Kings Cross Road, but then a rural health spa, surrounded by fields, and only accessible by foot or horse. It is very hard to visualise it today.

It is said that Bagnigge Wells was the summer home of Nell Gwyn's 'palace', in which she ably and sometimes wildly entertained Charles II and his entourage. At that time in the seventeenth century, the allegedly-restorative properties of the nearby springs, offshoots of the yet-pristine Fleet, had not been discovered, or at any rate were not commercially-valued for their curative properties, as they were to become in Georgian times. All was natural, quiet, enjoyed by the favoured, and remarkably distant from the urban London Town, difficult though that might be for us to imagine when contemplating the Kings Cross and Clerkenwell areas today.

Taking the waters by either bathing or drinking has, of course, been popular for millennia which is rather odd when one considers the fact that so much disease is water-borne. The instinctive human desire to immerse oneself in apparently cleansing and curative waters must have, itself, been a source of infection, if not fatal. The waters in Bath were closed to the public in 1978 after a girl died from a rare strain of meningitis which was linked to an amoeba found in the waters in which she had previously bathed.

Swimming in London in the eighteenth century was one activity which became very popular indeed among the wealthier. This resulted in the open-air pool, or even indoor pool in some grand houses, although chilliness seems to have been most favoured for bracing health reasons – possibly accounting for my own Edwardian grandmother's unshakeable assertion that if it hurts, it's doing you good. Rosina encouraged this stalwart attitude in her grandchildren, although I seem to recall that she was rather more keen on twentieth-century lifestyle benefits when it came to herself. Over 150 years before then, however, the seeds of a healthier lifestyle had already been sown if mostly, one cannot help but suspect, to counteract the overindulgence in food and drink so often found among the well-to-do. The 'swimming' pool, or dual-purpose civic reservoir, was hardly a new idea of course, as the earliest has been traced back to over 4,000 years ago in Pakistan, complete with a bitumen seal to prevent the water seeping away through the bricks.

A London gentleman of means interested in swimming might have visited the Peerless Pool, which was a commercial venture sited near the junction of modern-day Old Street and City Road, also in watery Clerkenwell. It was originally called the Perilous Pond because so many little lads had drowned in it, and it was a spring which naturally formed a large pool. We do not know how or why so many boys died, but it possibly had more to do with winter skating than summer swimming. However, in 1743 a local jeweller to 'the Quality', called William Kemp, turned his entrepreneurial gaze upon it and converted it into London's first proper swimming pool. He did not spare any expense, no doubt knowing well his target market. It was gentlemen only of course, and patrons wallowed in the up-market surroundings – for a price; £1.10s for an annual subscription, or 1s per day visit. Marble abounded, in the pathways and steps leading down into the pool, and in the changing-room which resembled a small temple. The pool had a gravelly bottom, added by William, which graded from about 3 to 5 feet which satisfied all clients both beginners and proficient, and the water was clear and, in summer, warm. Trees shaded the pool and young ladies could walk around it discreetly, but at a distance, eyeing up the bathers. There was also a separate pond for fishing, stocked with carp and bream, and eventually a library and a bowling green. Mr Kemp was a far-seeing pioneer of the leisure industry. It lasted until 1850 when it was drained and built over, doubtless because real estate in the rapidly-expanding central London was becoming far too valuable to be wasted on a swimming pool of roughly 170 by 108 feet. The site is memorialised, however, by the nearby Peerless and Bath streets. It has also featured in Georgette Heyer novels and *Death in the Peerless Pool*, a murder mystery by Deryn Lake set in the Regency.

There is evidence that Georgian men were using what we would call work-out routines to improve their physiques, including apparatus which involved weights on the end of a rope pulley, and prescribed and targeted exercises. Gymnastics or callisthenics have, of course, been well documented among the ancient Greeks, Spartans, Romans, Polynesians and Indians. At the time of such documentation these people were somewhat belligerent and, given the lower level of war technology, depended upon a ferociously-strong male physique. This did not apply to the average metropolitan Georgian man, however, despite the fact that they were still challenging each other to duels on occasion. Given their considerable interest in fashion, and their social competitiveness, one is inevitably driven to the suspicion that vanity might have been as equally motivating a force for exercise as health-consciousness. The Germans were hard at it in gymnasia, and the methodical Scandinavians were developing fitness routines. The British, it has to be admitted, rather preferred an element of fun to spice up their exercise. Games.

However, to understand the genesis of British sport and fitness, and that in the eighteenth century in particular, it is necessary, as usual, to journey back further in time. Much of sport derives from either war-like pursuits, or the substitution of sporting 'war' (with rules to prevent total mayhem) as a satisfying, skill-building, socially-bonding, and relatively-peaceful alternative.

Games and sports deriving from war included archery, fencing, wrestling and shooting; any team game which inevitably relied upon the interests of the individual being subordinated to that of the greater good; and those which rewarded spatial skills such as aiming, or just sheer endurance, such as racing. This covers just about anything we do today in the name of sport, but the genesis was fairly slow. In the Middle Ages archery was considered a mandatory skill as land-owning lords, who were in thrall to the king for one reason or another (financial or familial), were obliged to contribute troops to battle, and relied upon their servants or peasants for back-up. The latter had no alternative but to obey, unless they were too old, or female, or perhaps a brilliant and indispensable cook. The Highland Scots have been summoning the clans for tests of strength, skill and endurance for centuries.

By the eighteenth century, however, the British army comprising the English, Welsh, Irish and Scots, was not so dependent upon reluctantly-coerced amateurs in the lower ranks, and was building a cadre of fit professional soldiers who were being trained. At least, among the non-officer classes. Sadly, for those doing their best in the ranks, this more professional approach did not usually extend to the officers, most of whom still bought their commissions, although there were some notable exceptions who rose from the ranks, such as Sir William Robertson (1860–1933). Sir William was not a Georgian, but his story makes very clear that promotion on the grounds of sheer talent was somewhat rare. He remains our only soldier to have risen from Private to Field Marshal.

The assumption that the upper classes had natural leadership abilities endured until technology and the strategic demands of modern warfare, in the First World War, began to punch major holes in the idea. Many people may be somewhat startled to learn, though, that Sandhurst was not established until 1947, although nearby Aldershot was developed in 1854 during the Crimean War as the home of the British army and the foremost training camp for the British infantry. Military activity had existed there before, but the eighteenth century approach to military establishments did not appeal to the Victorians. It was, literally, a camp and attracted the usual hangers-on, including prostitutes, swindlers, and drinking dens. This was not the sort of environment in which to build fitness and discipline, and the Victorians set about building permanent barracks and churches, and banishing the camp-followers. And if that were not enough, Victoria and Albert took such a keen interest that they had built a wooden pavilion, which still exists, from which to keep a stern eye on things during their visits.

The nineteenth-century army understood the value of sport, of course, and drained land to establish playing fields, built the Maida Gymnasium, and commandeered the heathland surrounding Aldershot for athletic and military training purposes. The Georgians, however, did other and less sporting things in the area. The nearby road between Bagshot and Winchester was notorious for highway robberies, with Dick Turpin being reputed to have his headquarters in nearby Farnborough.

Sport in the eighteenth century, though, was here to stay and inevitably began to merge with the demands of building and maintaining a growing Empire. Anyone hoping to forge a career and reputation by venturing forth under challenging physical and environmental circumstances needed to be as fit as possible, and also demonstrate teamwork as well as leadership. Sport could help build this complex requirement, and the schools and government recognised this, even if some of the latter were often drinking port, making speeches, and lolling around in Gentlemen's clubs.

In the Middle Ages women, both rich and poor, often appear in illustrations playing ball games involving throwing, batting or kicking. An illuminated manuscript in the Bodleian Library in Oxford shows lively priests and nuns involved in a bat-and-ball game with the latter putting up a very spirited showing. In Scotland there was an annual football match involving single women versus married women. One can imagine that the men very much enjoyed cheering on their womenfolk on these occasions, although it was hardly ladies' soccer as we know it, and the lack of structure and rules meant it was a rather more unruly spectacle than we would countenance. Indeed, the more frequently-played male football matches often resulted in injury or even death, since the game roamed wildly over miles and for hours, between villages, and was generally subject to few rules or any effective supervision. Even in the Middle Ages the civil authorities were not best pleased. King James I of Scotland attempted to ban 'fute-ball' in 1424, but it is quite obvious that this did not work, and other rulers also made similarly futile attempts, including Edward II, Edward III, Henry IV and Oliver Cromwell. The authorities always encouraged physical prowess because any man could be called upon to fight for their lord or king at any time, but they preferred a more structured approach to honing the skills of battle, rather than mass brawling for fun and revenge. Many such games took place on Shrove Tuesday however, and were probably a way of letting off steam before the solemnity and privations of Lent began.

It is generally assumed that Britain, as the nation that exported organised sport all around the world, invented it, but this is unlikely. It got into its game-playing stride in the nineteenth century, inspired by the Victorian values of a healthy body, true grit, team spirit and fair play, as inculcated by the great public schools whose main task was to produce dutiful soldiers and administrators for the Empire. The Football Association was founded in 1863, complete with rules and a competitive structure, and the Lawn Tennis Association followed in 1888, which is perhaps why we associate the Victorians so much with organised sport; they liked rules and clubs, clubhouses and networking, big trophy cups, club colours and uniforms, and competitive leagues. This sort of dedicated organisation led, of course, to both national and international competition as communications and travel technology improved, and it is no coincidence that our most dangerous threats today in rugby and cricket come from vastly different countries in the old Empire, either the descendants of white ex-patriots or indigenous people. Their citizens obviously decided – possibly through gritted teeth – that useful though the legacy of the British Empire might be in terms of democracy and infrastructure, organised sport was certainly something to be adopted into their cultures. New Zealand, for example, is a country of only about 4½ million people, of whom just under 600,000 are estimated to be of Maori ethnicity. That 13 per cent, however, have always punched well above their weight when it comes to rugby – as is well known – but also cricket, which is not so well-known. These games were introduced by British settlers and missionaries of course but the Maoris, being of a robust physique and competitive spirit, were very keen. They had an 'official' Maori cricket team in the nineteenth century which was short-lived due to the fact that it always trounced the Pacific Ocean opposition, and was subsequently disbanded. This was an outrage from which Maori cricket never quite recovered, although efforts are now being made to revive it. New Zealand as a country, however, continues to benefit from the Maoris' great sporting prowess in their national teams, and to honour their contribution.

The West Indies, although comparatively small if scattered, now regularly astound everyone with tremendous cricketers and athletes. India, Pakistan, Sri Lanka and South Africa have no intention of allowing the British (well, alright, the English) to triumph at cricket ever again if they can help it, and that does not even begin to address the equally-virulent competitiveness of the Rugby 6-Nations competition, which is wholly European, but a precursor to the Rugby World Cup. If you think about it, who could ever have imagined that the French and Italians would ever have embraced English rugby? But they did.

Chasing, or playing with, a ball seems to be a motif which has occurred in every civilisation around the world. Everybody, from the ancient Egyptians onwards (and obviously before) knew that it was fun, but the early problem was that round balls were not easy to make, technologically. We know that early balls were fashioned from inflated or stuffed animal bladders, or clay for example, but they would not have been bouncy or long-lasting enough to truly develop or promote the skills of the players. Prototype ballgames, of which there were many, tended to be for young boys and girls. This is maybe why adult sports, on which everyone was understandably keen, tended to focus on wrestling, running, gymnastics, swimming, and fighting skills. None of these are essentially team sports. Team sports need a symbolic and durable object around which to harness the co-operative spirit and skills of the players. A ball. It rolls and bounces weirdly, and entrances nimble mammals from puppies and kittens to humans, via otters, cats, dogs, monkeys and apes, dolphins, orcas – and many more. The ball even intrigues some birds from either the very intelligent corvids (crows, magpies etc.), to the equally-clever parrot families like the New Zealand kea. Any creature smart enough to develop skills through play just loves a ball.

At the beginning of the Georgian era, ball games were widely played, including variants of soccer, but were not so very organised. A great favourite was cricket.

It is difficult to establish the origins of evidently similar bat-and-ball games from the medieval period onwards, but it is believed that cricket (creckett) was perhaps a foreign import in the sixteenth century, possibly from Flanders or France, and a children's game played mainly in the South East of England. One also supposes that fathers, then as now, took an interest in their sons' games and maybe endeavoured to bring some sort of orderly competitiveness to the business, if only to minimise injury and disorder among the young. After nearly 200 years of comparative mayhem, however, the eighteenth century began to get a firmer grip on the conduct of the sport even though the earlier newspaper accounts of the period generally concerned announcements of matches, wagers involved, and ensuing riots and bloodshed. But that is journalism. Away from such reports, however, cricket was becoming more orderly and structured largely because the ubiquitous and influential gamblers decided that the best way to improve their wagering chances was to form their own teams, and from the 1720s there are mentions of individual players becoming media 'stars'. In keeping with the usual Georgian gaming habits, the wagers sometimes reached truly colossal proportions, even topping 1,000 guineas on a single match, which must have made the occasion ridiculously tense.

Early cricket bats were more like hockey sticks because the ball was bowled along the ground, but the advent of 'flighted' delivery, which was faster and much more dangerous and exciting, heralded the straight bat, and positional fielders. Although the basic rules of cricket had existed for a long time, including dimensions of the field and wicket, the Duke of Richmond drew up Articles of Agreement in 1728 which were signed before particular games, although these unsurprisingly seem to have mostly covered aspects of wagering. In 1744, however, the Laws of Cricket were codified for the first time and modified in 1774 to cover such necessities as lbw, width of the bat, the addition of a middle stump, and the provision of two gentlemen umpires whose decisions were final. In 1787 the Marylebone Cricket Club (MCC) was founded at Lords.

There are many paintings of eighteenth-century cricket, most of which depict the use of the hockey-like stick, but one illustrating the straight bat shows a group of splendidly-gowned cricketing ladies in 1779, including the Countess of Derby, all wearing totally unsuitable shoes and enormous hats. These pictures show an instantly-recognisable game, usually devoid of the huge crowds which often attended them, and not a whiff of anything as ungentlemanly as gambling and alcohol-fuelled violence. There are no paintings of the pupils of Eton and Westminster who staggered off the pitch after a particularly bruising encounter which left several of them with 'black eyes and broken heads'. Nor, indeed, of one John Smith being carried off the pitch after being killed by a stone thrown from the crowd. Indeed, death by cricket was not just confined to commoners, if rumour is to be believed. The Prince of Wales, Frederick Louis, eldest son of George II, apparently died in 1751 a few days after being struck by a cricket ball in the chest, which is at least slightly more credible than the other touted alternative – a tennis ball. One has to note, however, that his doctors bled him, but he probably died of pneumonia.

The growing Georgian obsession with cricket as the 'national game' is also reflected in both the newspapers and popular literature. Contemporary journalism was evidently not for those with short attention spans or insufficient leisure time to read since, although announcements of matches might be a mere few hundred words, match reports could run to several thousand. The game also inspired much poetry, although that is perhaps being kind:

> His Grace the Duke of Dorset came, …
> Equall'd by few, he plays with glee,
> Nor peevish seeks for victory …
> And for unlike the Modern way
> Of blocking every ball at play,
> He firmly stands with bat upright,
> And strikes with athletic might,
> Sends forth the ball across the mead,
> And scores six notches for the deed.
>
> John Burn (circa 1773)

His Grace obviously played to the crowd rather than for safety and was, no doubt, revered for doing so. Except, maybe, by some of his more apprehensive backers who feared that his buccaneering style might lead to an early demise.

But cricket was not the only emerging national game. Soccer (football), for previously-mentioned socio-economic reasons, did not attract such huge amounts in wagering, but it still won in the end by sheer force of the volume of participants and supporters. The upper classes, in public schools, also largely forsook the game in the nineteenth century in favour of Rugby

Union and other games which required more investment in expensive infrastructure, including golf, tennis, squash, and athletics. Hardly academic, but still interesting, are the books of a writer called Frank Richards, who wrote the Billy Bunter stories in the Edwardian period. Bunter, himself, was utterly inept at sport due to his hopeless physique, even though his more keen, nimble and skillful classmates were, such as Bob Cherry and Harry Wharton. Their notable and celebrated cricketing Indian princeling friend, Hurree Jamset Ram Singh, was affectionately called 'Darkie'. Never mind. It was a long time ago, and it was fiction, even if inspired by fact.

Prior to the eighteenth century there were many notions about exercise which we would regard as fallacious and which began to be refuted due to scientific and medical advances, such as weight training slowing down runners, and aerobic exercise not being good for either women or seniors. Women and seniors in the eighteenth century, however, were not a profitable target market for entrepreneurs who spotted a sporting chance for profit. Men were, and are lured to gyms, boxing clubs, fencing classes, target practice, and athletic clubs.

The visitor to a Georgian sporting event who intends to participate will, however, need to realise that his fellow sportsmen may well take a much more rumbustious approach than he is used to. It would therefore be wise to consider the Georgian health options available in the case of injury before cheerfully joining in. We are used to a trip to A & E in the event of an accident. That will not happen in the eighteenth century.

Chapter Six

Behaving Properly

The eighteenth century was an Age of Etiquette. We appreciate good manners of course, but ours are more 'natural' than stylized since we mostly place the emphasis on consideration for others, even if mobile phone usage does often seem rather resistant to courtesy.

Manners have always been important as a rational way of oiling human interactions, making sure that the proletarians show respect to their betters, and as a method of discouraging social climbing. William Wykeham (1320–1404), who founded Winchester public school and New College, Oxford, chose for his motto 'Manners Makyth Man'. Some people might consider this a somewhat limited ambition, but the Bishop probably knew exactly what he was suggesting since he was actually founding educational establishments for clever but poorer, and ordinary, boys. He knew that brains were not enough, and that one of the tasks of his school was to apply a social veneer that might just bluff his lads through to success. He, himself, was the son of a relatively poor man, John Long, from Wickham in Hampshire. For over 600 years his far-sighted educational legacy has lived on, although his own foundations were hijacked over the centuries as Winchester and Oxford became the preserve of the wealthy and aristocratic. His recognition that intellectual talent could be found in the most unlikely of places was not, of course, so very unusual. Henry VIII placed great faith and trust in the very able Thomas Cromwell, his Chancellor and the son of an alcoholic and abusive blacksmith, and bitterly regretted being manoeuvred into eventually executing him through the machinations of scheming aristocrats. Master Cromwell, bravely, did the decent thing at his execution by praising the king who was sending him to his death, before being eventually despatched by a (reputedly) drunken and consequently incompetent axeman. Not being an aristocrat, he did not warrant the mercy of a skilled French swordsman, there being privilege even in death.

Two hundred years on, the aristocratic Georgians were increasingly faced with the emergence of a growing and ambitious middle class, both financially and socially. This presented a problem, since the business talents of the latter were undoubtedly needed as the Colonies and trade burgeoned. One did not, however, necessarily want to socialise with them, and certainly not intermarry with them. The trouble was that these people had money and were socially observant in terms of material wealth; they could buy the same clothes and afford servants to keep up the lifestyle. Furthermore, they were beginning to show signs of considerable political and business clout. What was needed was what we would now understand as a 'barrier to market entry' and that was, of necessity, a social one; ways of behaving that only those born to the coronet or established inheritance would know, and ignorance of which would become immediately obvious – and humiliating. One only has to think of Mr Darcy's first proposal of marriage to Elizabeth Bennet in Jane Austen's *Pride and Prejudice* to realise how deeply such attitudes ran, and how reasonable they seemed to a wealthy suitor in Regency times, if not to the perfectly respectable Elizabeth:

> In vain have I struggled. It will not do. My feelings will not be repressed. You must allow me to tell you how ardently I admire and love you …
> His sense of her inferiority – of its being a degradation – of the family obstacles which judgment had always opposed to inclination, were dwelt on with a warmth which seemed due to the consequence he was wounding, but was very unlikely to recommend his suit.

One man who understood and anticipated this problem, and who allegedly imported the French word 'etiquette' into Britain, was Philip Stanhope, the 4th Earl of Chesterfield (1694–1773), whose family life was rather extraordinary. He is remembered not only for his diplomatic and political services to his country, but also for his letters to his illegitimate but loved son, Philip, on the topic of manners and society. The earl's domestic life was somewhat complicated, and the younger Philip's mother was, predictably enough, a French governess in the household. Although comprising over four-hundred letters in thirty years, these were only published after Chesterfield's death by his (belatedly-wed) daughter-in-law, Eugenia Stanhope, and the mother of his two born-illegitimate grandsons (another Philip, and George). The younger Philip, and partner of Eugenia, does not seem to have been very receptive to the lessons from his slightly disappointed father, and it was only after the death of the 4th Earl in 1773 that Eugenia published the letters, in

1774, receiving the fabulous sum of 1,500 guineas. It took her less than a year, however, which does suggest that she'd been giving the matter some thought. This was doubtless prompted by the fact that her husband had died six years earlier, and she was left nothing in Chesterfield's will when he died, despite his providing generously for her two sons. It may seem rather odd to us that the progenitor of the many books of instructions on etiquette, which sold prolifically for over a century and allowed Eugenia to die a wealthy woman, should have sprung from a family in which nearly every natural heir was technically illegitimate and confusingly named Philip. But Chesterfield was an aristocrat, although that did not prevent the (upstart) powers in the land from demonstrating their disapproval of all these extra-marital shenanigans by declining to advance the careers of the 'bastard' scions of this confusing family, no matter how much the old earl paid or networked.

Books on behaviour, or etiquette, were big business in the eighteenth and nineteenth centuries as a result of social-climbing, and are legion. It is thought by some social historians that only the ambitions of the middle-classes could have resulted in such a boom, and also the consequent democracy that we now take for granted. So many of those making fortunes in the dreaded 'trade' plotted to storm the ramparts of privilege, aided by books and magazine articles on conduct and manners, that the power of the socially-besieged aristocrats slowly began to fall. Not merely because of that, of course, but it was a positive feedback loop to drive what the aristocracy feared most; the advancement of the clever and educated, but disdained, middle-classes. Every time the real toffs adopted a new way of dressing or behaving, the burgeoning media immediately informed the middle-classes how it should be done, and they paid close attention, especially if it affected their children.

Understandably enough, quite a lot of ink was devoted to the topic of how to induce children to behave both decorously and bravely either to the station in life in which they were raised, or that to which their parents' aspired. It is often assumed that 250 years ago, childhood was shorter (in terms of the allowances made for youth) and more brutal, with corporal punishment to the forefront of instruction. This is quite likely to have been the experience of a child of wealthy parents, under the sway of insufficiently-supervised tutors or governesses, and sent away to public school from a very young age. The less privileged seem to have led lives not so very dissimilar to our own families, emotionally. Some were indeed abusive, but most seemed loving and caring and wanting to do the best they could for their many offspring, given their economic and educational circumstances, and the distressingly high mortality rate among young children. In burgeoning Georgian Britain, however, it did seem the possibility of self-advancement, no matter how difficult or grim, was feasible.

On the continent of Europe and even beyond, however, it seemed that only bloody revolution would suffice. In Britain though, the Protestant pulpit somehow managed to reconcile both a work ethic driven self-improvement, and humbly knowing one's place. During both the eighteenth and nineteenth centuries the British aristocracy feared revolution, but it seems the lower orders were too busy trying to improve their own lot in life to organise uprisings, tumbrils and grim executions. In fact, revolutions were happening all over ... except here. We know about the American and French revolutions because they affected us considerably, but the poor and un-enfranchised were rising up elsewhere. Latin America was stoking turmoil against their European oppressors, as was Haiti, an island dependent upon the labour of understandably recalcitrant African slaves for its European masters' wealth. The Balkans (Poland mainly) were chafing against both Russian and Prussian rule, and Vietnam was embroiled in difficulties not helped by the fact that most protagonists were called Nguyen, which made allegiance rather problematic. Many of the military encounters took place at the beginning of the nineteenth century, but the seeds were sown much earlier in the eighteenth century.

Literate Georgians could read about such things in newspapers, but had no way of knowing if it were true, since news was both sensationally-presented and time-lapsed. The instinctive reaction of the aristocratic was nervousness about the thoughts and inclinations of the masses upon whose labour and deference they so depended. The more philanthropic among them must have felt confused as, after all, they were kind and considerate to their minions, albeit within acceptable social limits. However, it was observed in the late nineteenth century that the trouble with extending literacy to the poor was that, as soon as they were taught to read the Bible, the next book they had clutched in their hands was Karl Marx's *Das Kapital*. This can hardly have been literally true, of course, but does illustrate the apprehension about the education of the lower classes, which began in the eighteenth century. Rather more Georgians than we might suspect were eagerly learning to read, even if it was only to be able to read the Scriptures as their teachers hoped. But literacy opened up a whole new philosophical and historical world.

The Rev. Wheatley doing penance for adultery. (*Artist: Unknown. Source: The Newgate Calendar*)

Hayward waltzing with a Lady of Quality. (*Artist: Unknown. Source: The Newgate Calendar*)

East Indiaman. (*Creator: Samuel Prout (undated). Source: Yale University Centre for British Art*)

The Royal Sport, Pit Ticket. (*Artist: Unknown. Source: Yale University Centre for British Art*)

Games at Vauxhall: playing at cricket. (*Print by Guillaume Benoist, undated. Source: Yale University Centre for British Art*)

Dr.Graham's Cold Earth & Warm Mud Bathing. (*Artist: Thomas Rowlandson, undated. Source: Yale University Centre for British Art*)

An Audience at Drury Lane Theatre. (*Artist: Thomas Rowlandson (1756–1827), undated. Source: Yale University Centre for British Art*)

Mrs. Yates in the Character of Medea. (*Artist: unknown, after 1771. Source: Yale University Centre for British Art*)

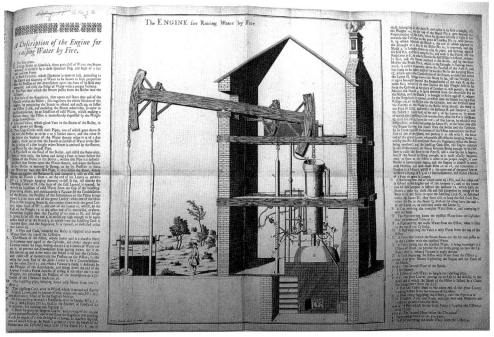

A Steam Engine for raising Water by Fire. (*Author: Sutton Nichols. Source: The British Library*)

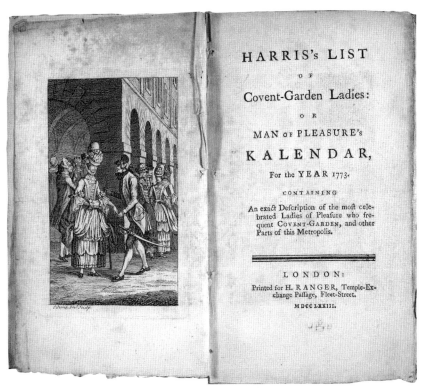

Harris's List of Covent Garden Ladies (prostitutes). (*Author: unknown; designer Samuel Derrick, printed in London from 1757–1769. Source: The British Library*)

Popular Entertainments in 1778. (*Printer: unknown. Source: The British Library*)

On MONDAY next, Dec. 31, 1787.

HORSEMANSHIP
By the inimitable Master SMITH, Mr. HANDY, and Others.

The UNICORN,
Will be exhibited for the fourth Time.

A Jockey Hornpipe,
Or a Trip to Newmarket Races.
By Mr. Franklin, and four other Performers.

A NEW BALLETTE,
Composed by Mr. SPOZZI

A MINUET,
By Mr. SPOZZI and Mrs. STEVENS.

ROPE DANCING,
By the Inimitable Troop of Female Rope Dancers from *Paris*.

OW WOW Song, by Mr. Johannot.

HORSE VAULTING by Sieur HANDY.

The Tumblers Morris
Composed by Mr. LAWRENCE.

Slack Rope Vaulting in full Swing.

WIRE DANCING.
Mr. FRANKLIN will carry a Boy on his Shoulders in the
Attitude of FLYING MERCURY.
The Horsemanship will end with

The Taylor's Journey to Brentford.
To conclude (with Improvements) a Pantomime, called

Harlequin Restored,
Or the POWER of MAGIC.

Tickets to be had of Mr. FRANKLIN and of Mr. SWINNEY, Printer.

Entertainments at Bartholomew Fair. (*Creator: unknown. Source: The British Library*)

Bethlem Hospital (Bedlam), the final destination of The Rake. (*Artist: William Hogarth, The Rake's Progress. Source: The British Library*)

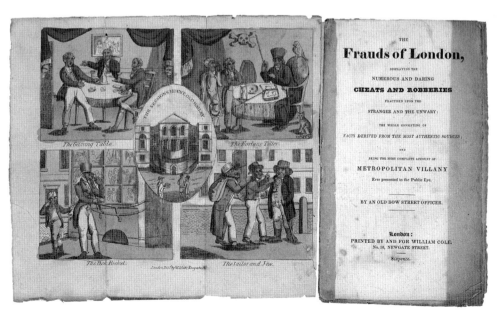

The Frauds of London. (*Author: An Old Bow Street Officer, illustrator unknown, pub. William Cole. Source: The British Library*)

Gin Lane. (*Artist: William Hogarth, 1751. Source: The British Library*)

GIN LANE.

The Party Breaking Up and Qua Genus Breaking Down; 18th Century traffic accident. (*Artist unknown. Source: The British Library*)

Rather more perplexing is the number of books on good manners which were aimed at churchmen. One would not have suspected the clergy to have been so very rude, but apparently some were. This is probably because, in the eighteenth century, parish livings were in the gift of the landowners, and doubtless they expected their appointees to be suitably humble. Many churchmen, however, were the younger sons of the wealthy, probably did not take kindly to being patronised, and had been educated to deliver rousing sermons about sin, especially pride and adultery. Here, one is irresistibly reminded of the clergyman Mr Collins, in Jane Austen's *Pride and Prejudice*, who had a nauseatingly grovelling relationship with his patron, Lady Catherine de Bourgh. He certainly knew his place, and had probably read *The Rules of Good Deportment for Church Officers* (1730), which goes into extraordinary detail about what both God and the church patrons expected. The Preface informs us that:

All Churchmen should shine in their Character, and be charming in their Conversation; their Manners polished; their Language refin'd, far above the vulgar Standard. They should perform every Act of Life with its proper Graces. Men, in such a Station, that are rude in their Behaviour, make but an unlovely Figure among the Polite.

Jonathan Swift, that admirable eighteenth-century satirist, published his own essay on how to make polite conversation, advocating the employment of trite clichés. This, of course, was not intended to be taken seriously, although some naïve people apparently did so. One Lord Orrery, whose public endorsement of Swift's 'advice', was smuggled into the latter's diatribe about people's public behaviour and the boredom of formal social gatherings, attracted considerable ridicule.

A great deal of the advice dispensed by such manuals on etiquette might be quite familiar to anyone today who has had to endure dinner parties or alcohol-fuelled receptions with strangers, some of whom might be socially or financially important. Basically, the main advice was to look one's best, not to drink too much, steer clear of politics and religion, and never tell jokes. Then, as now, this is probably sound advice for those wanting to fit in. But was it good advice for those who want to stand out from the crowd? Some Georgians decided that it was not, but they are now remembered more for their iconoclasm than their social success, and there were quite a few men and women who took quite a chance on being social renegades. Such eccentricity was, of course, accepted among the elite but certainly not among the aspiring middle classes.

Unpleasant though they sometimes sound, one cannot help but feel a bit sorry for the Georgian aristocracy fighting a losing battle against brains, time, and progress. One should not feel too sorry, though, as vestiges of this attitude have persisted well into our own times. Alan Clark (1928–1999), who was a Tory MP and who had academically distinguished parents and a stellar education, but no real aristocratic connections, was moved to remark snobbishly about fellow-MP, Michael Heseltine, that he was the sort of person 'who had to buy all his own furniture ...'. Mr Clark was, however, an historian, amateur satirist, and general all-round mischief-maker, so perhaps one should not take this too seriously. Nonetheless, this is an interesting vestige of the social conflict that bedevilled the eighteenth and nineteenth centuries and, who knows, possibly yet our own? Even if our media-driven celebrity culture is somewhat different from previous eras, our own desires to emulate whichever role model we decide upon is probably very little different. Gleaming Hollywood teeth anyone – at vast cost, considerable pain, and high maintenance?

By Victorian times, preserving bloodlines and social ties had become almost an obsession among the upper classes, despite the rise of the middle classes. This lasted until the beginning of the last century when the cost of keeping up vast estates and the appropriate lifestyle, and the ravages of Asquith's Inheritance Tax in 1914, meant that the aristocracy began to look more favourably upon marriages between their noble sons and the daughters of respectable middle-class captains of industry, or even rich Americans. The Jerome sisters from Boston, Jenny and Leonie, settled here in 1873 with their social-climbing mother. Jenny married Lord Randolph Churchill, and became the mother of Winston, while Leonie married Sir John Leslie, an Anglo-Irish baronet with great land holdings.

Now, however, it is time for practical advice for the time-traveller on how to survive, undetected, among the Georgians, in terms of speech and personal conduct.

Greetings and Salutations

This will be an area fraught with potential social gaffes. Rituals of salutation have always existed in every society and involve a delicate interplay of acknowledgement, recognition, respect and deference depending on status, age and gender. The most universally-recognised gesture of unthreatening acknowledgement among all humans is merely eye-contact followed by briefly-raised eyebrows, an upward tilt of the head and, maybe, just the merest hint of a smile. This seemingly hard-wired response has broken the ice in first encounters between strangers throughout all societies, and serves to suggest that aggression may be deferred – pending further and cautious interaction. In complex and status-conscious societies, however, this ancient instinct was obviously not enough to preserve and reinforce the pecking orders of civilisation, so further rituals were necessary. It seems that every possible gesture, posture and verbal greeting has been formalised somewhere, from total prostration to totally ignoring someone.

In eighteenth century emerging cities, like London, where the poor and the aspiring middle-classes would inevitably interact with their betters in ever more complex situations, from being servants to lawyers for example, etiquette became very important. None of us will ever get it absolutely right, but here is a brief guide to not getting it catastrophically wrong in better-off circles.

Gentlemen:

- Always wear a hat outside the home, but doff it instantly when admitted to another house.
- Wear gloves, especially when being introduced to the opposite sex. No skin-on-skin interaction please, and do not presume to press a female's gloved hand unless she offers it first.
- You may sit to take refreshments, but must rise and bow when someone of an equal or superior rank enters the room, of either gender.
- At social gatherings you will be expected to dance sedately and elegantly, but not more than three times with any young lady to whom you are not engaged to be married.
- Ladies are considered both feeble-minded and worthy of gentlemanly behaviour, so you may have a difficult line to tread when confronted with smart, determined and scheming women who have unmarried daughters.

Ladies:

A rigorous guide to behaviour can be found in *The Whole Duty of a Woman*: Or, *An Infallible Guide to the Fair Sex. CONTAINING Rules, Directions, and Observations, for their Conduct and Behaviour through all Ages and Circumstances of Life, as Virgins, Wives or Widows*. This was printed for one T. Read in London in 1737 and owned by a Sarah Stack who, one imagines, must have felt both anxious and depressed. (Harvard University free E-book). As one might expect, the poor virgins are subject to the most trenchant strictures concerning conduct. It eased up somewhat as they progressed through life, just so long as mourning was correctly observed and they had not irretrievably blotted their copybook on the way. Allowances were made to cantankerous old ladies. The book begins in a very lofty style:

> The two grand Elements, essential to the Virgin State are Modesty and Obedience ... Her Look, her Speech, her whole Behaviour should own an humble Distrust of herself; she is to look on herself but as a Novice, a Probationer in the World, and must take this time rather to Learn and Observe, than to dictate and prescribe. Indeed, there is scarce any thing looks more indecent, than to see a young maid too forward and confident in her Talk.

Well, that certainly put the young ladies in their place, but Georgian women were not quite so easily dismissed. Many of the wealthier educated themselves beyond needlework and music in their indulgent father's libraries, hosted salons where they could discuss 'masculine' issues with their polite male guests, and ruthlessly exploited the principle of 'the power behind the throne' with their husbands.

Much of this has been culled from various books and articles on eighteenth-century etiquette, but it cannot possibly all be true of course. Knowing today's young, and remembering one's own youth, makes it certain that books on etiquette written by the married and respectable were not universally observed, except by the timid or socially-constrained. Many lads and girls in the emerging industrial society managed to outrage their parents, both rich and poor, and sometimes got their own way, whether wisely or not. Meeting the opposite sex, however, was somewhat regulated by parents, whether either of higher or lower class.

Dancing will be a tricky business for the time-traveller as it was stylized and formal, and of considerable duration by our standards. However, help will be at hand from the Georgian dancing master, who was nearly always from the lower classes. He, and later she, were there to coach those who either did not know how it was done, or were somewhat clumsy and inelegant in their skills and needed to perfect their movements and gestures for upwardly-mobile reasons. Samuel Pepys, in the seventeenth century, who was hardly a faithful husband, became rather jealous of his wife's dancing master and wrote sourly about it from the very beginning, and continued to complain about the time spent in flirting and laughing during these lessons, '… merrily practising to dance, which my wife hath begun to learn this day of Mr. Pembleton, but I fear will hardly do any great good at it, because she is conceited that she do well already, though I think no such thing.'

Hogarth caricatured the dancing master whose income, one assumes, rested on his ability to coax his pupils through ever more complicated and possibly embarrassing routines, necessitating even more lessons. Hogarth's learners are not altogether happy, from what one can gather from the prints.

Many dances were imported from France, that country which insisted on incredibly complex etiquette in its Royal Court. The British at first embraced the decency of the Minuet and the Gavotte and other formal dances, but not too long afterwards began to be interested in lively indigenous folk dancing, and what we would now know as tap-dancing. Georgian men made quite a clatter with their shoes, and the ladies had musical talents which did not go unnoticed as they were very impressive on the harp and the cello particularly, despite the Georgian male tendency to ignore them in formal settings, if not in the salon. This persisted into the twentieth century, when those first ladies to make it into an orchestra, the harpists, had to wear tuxedos and sit at the back disguised as men in suits.

You can only laugh.

Chapter Seven

Law & Order

Only the most assiduous of twenty-first century researchers would fancy making sense of the Georgian notion of justice or doing time in gaol merely to empathise with the miseries of law-breakers, so it would be wise to know how to stay out of trouble. In many respects this should not be too difficult since it is obvious that one was not allowed to wander around murdering people or robbing them with impunity, but there were snares for the unwary which could carry unpleasant penalties.

George I, for example, was evidently a very strict animal breeder as he announced severe punishment for any commoner heedless enough to allow their domestic animal to mate with one of his exalted royal pets. This can hardly have affected many people, of course, but the mere fact that it existed in law as a culpable offence attests to the often random, and top-down, nature of law making. In fact, this law has never been repealed, so it would still be wise today to keep your dog on a lead if walking it in Windsor Great Park and a corgi frolics into view. Equally bizarre, to our minds, might be the medieval laws still extant in the eighteenth century, including the prohibition against wearing a suit of armour in Parliament, which has also never been repealed. Even some of those laws enacted in Georgian times we would find redundant if not extraordinary, such as the death sentence being an option for impersonating an Egyptian, or appearing with a sooty face (Black Act 1723). Our eighteenth century ancestors, despite the Enlightenment, were still in a muddle about witchcraft for example, which they strangely endorsed in that Statute Law in 1752 concerning women entrapping men into matrimony, despite having sensibly repealed the 'offence' over a decade earlier. Past centuries, though, do not have a monopoly on puzzling laws. Since 1998, it has been specifically illegal in the UK to cause a nuclear explosion, which is an event one would have thought to have been covered well enough by other already existing laws.

However, compared to our highly regulated and surveilled society, the 'Long Arm of the Law' was surprisingly short in the eighteenth century, if disconcertingly capricious. In fact, most prosecutions for 'lower-level' crime or misdemeanours were private and brought by the victims themselves, and the results were often unfathomable to the modern mind. People were mostly either freed, pardoned, fined, transported … or hanged. Confinement in a gaol usually preceded a trial to prevent either re-offending or flight, and was not generally a form of long-term punishment if found guilty, presumably because imprisonment cost public money. From this follows the inevitable generalisation that if you had money, you got away with it and paid the fine but, if you were poor, you might well be in danger of paying with your life. Bringing a private prosecution, however, was usually tedious, expensive and uncertain, as everybody on both sides of the law very well knew.

To begin with, there was no police force as we would understand it in the eighteenth century, dedicated to the detection of crime and the pursuit of offenders. Civil government, particularly in the burgeoning towns, did provide some deterrence to crime in the form of magistrates, 'constables', nightwatchmen, churchwardens, beadles, or surveyors of the highways. Some of these people were paid, but constables generally were not and it was, in fact, often the duty of householders to undertake the task in rotation for periods of up to a year. Their role was to apprehend anyone accused of a felony and bring them before a justice of the peace, and to assist in keeping the peace, but nobody expected them to investigate a crime. All citizens had a duty to pursue a criminal if a hue and cry were raised by a shout of 'Stop, thief!' Witnesses to a crime were obliged to report it, but the onus of prosecution – and its attendant costs – was on the victim, and that caused a lot of problems. There were exceptions, of course, such as high treason, espionage, murder, or firing His Majesty's dockyards (Protection of Dockyards Act 1772). The only person actually executed for the latter seems to have been one John (the Painter) Aitken (1752–1777) a slightly crazed individual who developed an obsession with the power of the Royal Navy after spending two years in the American colonies. However, his was a criminal career variously involving being a highwayman, robber, shoplifter, burglar and, on one occasion, a rapist near Basingstoke. He admitted that he was ashamed of the latter.

Since there was no investigatory authority, anyone who was robbed, for example, had to establish the identity of the thief either by catching them at it, or relying on other witnesses, and then summon a possibly-reluctant constable to do his duty. If the suspect was successfully apprehended a magistrate would then decide, usually with a jury which probably had better things to do, whether there was a case to answer, and whether or not to hold the accused in custody pending any trial, rather like today's American Grand Jury arraignment system. All this, in itself, was a procedure of some difficulty and doubt, so it is hardly surprising that most people, unless the stolen items were of considerable value, thought it much easier just to give the thief a beating if caught in the act, or otherwise to make sure as many people as possible knew about his or her identity. If it was judged that there was a case to answer, the outraged victim then had to decide whether to proceed with the prosecution and, here, the money involved began to seriously mount. Victims had to pay for the administrative cost of the trial, and the expenses of any witnesses attending – not to mention the general expectation of a reward for their testimony which can only have compromised justice – and all possibly without any prospect of restoration of property or compensation in the form of a fine. Very little, indeed, save revenge. Small wonder, then, that there was little point in pursuing an impecunious criminal or petty crime. To compound this disadvantageous cost-benefit equation, there was the fact that judges and juries were also very aware of it, and alive to the possibility of corruption or a miscarriage of justice. They were often surprisingly reluctant to convict on merely the evidence of the victim, and often not much more inclined to believe witnesses who they suspected of being in it for a reward, either in terms of money or influence, especially if the penalty might be hanging or transportation. A surprising number of death sentences were mitigated. This is rather heartening when one considers that juries were comprised of men of some means, who might reasonably expect to be the most likely victims of crime themselves.

In Georgian England there were more than 200 capital offences, although far fewer where such a sentence was mandatory, which suggests that the Georgians believed in both deterrence and the possible benefits of mercy. But there were problems in reconciling the two as, indeed, there still are today and probably always will be. Remember the remark of the seventeenth-century George Savile, 1st Marquess of Halifax, who was as handy with a neat aphorism as his French contemporary, the Duc de la Rochefoucauld. 'Men are not hang'd for stealing Horses, but that Horses may not be stolen.'

The very basis of the law, however, made justice a difficult thing to both comprehend and administer. The foundation of the law was the ancient and cumulative Common Law which is made by judges, sitting in courts, applying the principles of legal precedent. This means that justice should theoretically be both public and consistent. The problem, of course, is that social and economic circumstances changed as the centuries went by as, indeed, did people's views, knowledge, and perceptions. Another rather dubious assumption inherent in Common Law is that judges are both incorruptible and wise, although nobody has ever really assumed any such thing, as is witnessed by the appeals system to either the monarch or his representatives. Common law was administered after the Norman Conquest through three central courts, namely the Court of King's Bench, the Court of Common Pleas, and the Exchequer. A dissatisfied litigant or hard done-by criminal could apply to the king for a remedy or mercy or, later, the King's Council.

Statute law – that enacted by Parliament over the Centuries – has always been rather a catch-up sort of business. The great and the good, the wise and the mighty – and the self-interested – have always scurried around legally trying either to amend outdated laws to suit the circumstances of their times, or to protect themselves and their property.

Georgian statute law emanated from the Crown, via Parliament, as had been customary for centuries. One king who gained a particularly great reputation for legal fairness and innovation until the Welsh Tudors disparaged him for political reasons was, surprisingly to many perhaps, the last English king, Richard III who was, of course, killed at the Battle of Bosworth Field in 1485. When not allegedly plotting the disappearance of his nephews in the Tower, he applied himself to jurisprudence during the brief seven-hundred and seventy-seven days of his reign (so much for lucky seven). Sir Frances Bacon, Lord Chancellor of England from 1618 to 1621, said of him 'A good lawmaker for the ease and solace of the common people.'

That Richard III was serious about this aspect of his rule can be realised by the fact that his Parliament sat for only thirty days in 1484, yet managed to pass (at his regal and powerful behest no doubt) no fewer than fifteen public statutes, all of which were compassionate, commendable, far-seeing, and almost revolutionary for the fifteenth century. And not to his own personal advantage.

He was particularly aware of bribery and corruption amongst 'officials' and, indeed, the Crown, and outlawed 'benevolences', which were compulsory taxes or payments exacted by sovereigns without the consent of Parliament. He introduced the system of bail and thus, by extension, considerably bolstered the principle of innocent until proven guilty; he insisted that jurors should be well-off land-owners (because, hopefully, they'd be less open to bribery); he decreed that land transfers should be made more transparent; and he attempted to limit the powers of the traditional and subsequently abused 'Piepowder' courts, which were running out of control. Their original remit had been merely to regulate fairs, but was now far more widely applied. It is on record that, in 1483, he instructed the Court of Pleas should 'hear the bills, requests and supplications, of poor persons.' He also thought that the new technology of printing books was a very good idea for the purposes of education and the dissemination of knowledge, and that economic tariffs were fair enough to protect the nation's trade. In medieval times, of course, he might have been both guilty of infanticide *and* be celebrated for being a good king to his people, although many historians now think such a duality is rather unlikely. His death caused considerable sorrow in the city of York:

> King Richard late mercifully reigning upon us was thrugh grete treason of the duc of Northefolk and many othre that turned ayenst hyme, with many othre lordes and nobilles of this north parties, was pitiously slane and murdred to the grete hevynesse of this citie.
>
> York House Books, Vol 1 p. 368–69

But this was in the fifteenth century, over 250 years before the Georgians, which makes it even more notable how very long it takes for societies to evolve towards justice and democracy. Magna Carta was reluctantly signed by King John in 1215. It was hardly a blueprint of democracy for the people as the enforcing rebel barons were only concerned with their own rights and affairs and, anyway, neither side seems to have had much intention of honouring their commitments. It was re-written several times, and only went into statute law in 1297 in a revised form, which was a concession granted by Edward I in return for more baronial taxes for the royal coffers, largely in order to wage war on the Welsh and the Scots. Freedom has never been free.

Although such inequitable justice was customary, however, this did not strike all Georgians as fair, particularly where the poor or destitute children were concerned, and they knew the law was not protecting the vulnerable. We credit the Victorian philanthropists and social activists with the great reforming conscience, but this is unjust. For one thing, the Victorians were rather preoccupied with the concept of the 'deserving poor', and although this at least was a start, they also had better communications due to developing technologies in printing, railways and roads, an impressive postal system, and improving domestic lighting. The latter may seem an odd contributor to social and legal reform, but the guttering eighteenth-century candlelight and the quill were rather less satisfactory companions to the tasks of studying, reading, and writing at the end of the long working day. The Georgians, or some of them, had real social concerns, but with less ability to effectively campaign, recruit support, and influence the mighty, and often heedless, law-makers. Georgian social reformers, philosophers, women, and the wealthy who had time, money and brains, motivated their Victorian successors who would indeed succeed in gradually changing their own, and our, world.

Georgian philanthropists include Captain Thomas Coram who, when retired in his fifties, became very distressed about the number of starving, diseased and abandoned babies and toddlers in the streets of London. He wanted to establish a foundling hospital to care for them, which did not discriminate against the illegitimate (which most of them were, of course). Despite having good connections to the ruling classes he found this very difficult until George II acceded to the throne and Queen Caroline lent her support to his efforts. In 1739, after years of exhausting campaigning, Coram succeeded in getting the king to sign a Royal Charter, which guaranteed State recognition, to care for the 'education and maintenance of exposed and deserted young children.' William Hogarth was a founding governor of the hospital, and Handel also supported the cause by giving benefit performances. Several artists donated works to be hung on the walls of the hospital and, by doing so, established the idea of the art gallery as people flocked to see them.

Another notable philanthropist was Jonas Hanway who, in 1756, established The Marine Society to aid recruitment and improve conditions for sailors in the Royal Navy. He was also instrumental in founding the Magdalen Hospital to rehabilitate prostitutes. One might (uncharitably) suspect that one interest inevitably led to the other.

The most famous social reformer of the age was William Wilberforce (1759–1833), the deeply religious Member of Parliament for Hull. He did not begin adult life as a virtuous man however and was, in fact, described by some as 'dissolute' until he became a Christian evangelist. One is irresistibly reminded of St Augustine's alleged prayer: 'Grant me chastity and continence, dear Lord … but not yet.' Wilberforce's outstanding contribution to social reform was his campaign against slavery, of course, but he also worked tirelessly to improve the conditions for workers in factories. These social innovations were all charitable enterprises, not state-initiated, and depended upon public subscription and the support of influential and wealthy people. Enough of them stepped up to the plate to make a very considerable difference, which would leave a legacy of reform and statute law from which we, and others, benefit to this day.

In the eighteenth century, law-making was still generally linked to religious beliefs and sanctions, and to the mystique of royalty, despite the best efforts of philosophers like David Hume and political thinkers like Thomas Paine. The established political parties then, and thus those who held power and controlled the emerging mainstream media, were the Whigs and Tories. As a generalisation, the Whigs were aristocratic, and the Tories were empowered by the emerging middle classes of merchants, empire-building entrepreneurs, lawyers, and sometimes the younger sons of the landed gentry who were obliged, for one reason or another, to earn a living or at least do something to keep their allowance from their often-exasperated parents. Many of these younger sons, however, were clever and active young men who had a genuine interest in science, astronomy, philosophy, mathematics – and the law – and who were in a position to research, think, and influence. Not all were so talented, however, and the eighteenth century saw the rise of the 'remittance man', who was packed off to the colonies to fend for himself in return for an allowance. Provided he never came back. Some of them ultimately did rather well, though. We would call it tough love.

So the eighteenth and nineteenth centuries benefited from a particular sort of person, now largely lost to our society; that of the well-off, well-educated, energetic, and basically under-employed young man. Many of these were the younger sons of the wealthy who often had to choose between the army or the church for an occupation as very few fathers wanted immature, idle, and spoilt sons loafing around dissolutely, squandering the family money, and impregnating unsuitable local girls.

The more adventurous or less academic usually bought a commission in the army, and from among their ranks came some, essentially practical, men who devoted their ample leisure time (when not campaigning abroad) to engineering, or other useful experimental projects involving explosives, guns, bullets, death etc. Their brothers at home, who chose the church, often had even more leisure time. They were usually not trained in matters of divinity since the basic requirement for a Church of England sinecure was merely a degree, which was not hard to come by if you were well-off and had even a moderate taste for some study, and family connections. In addition to whatever family allowance the budding rector or vicar received, he would also benefit from the tithes. We tend to assume that churches, 200 years ago, were simply heaving with regular and devout congregants, but there is little evidence for this. People wanted to be christened, married and buried by the church, but were not so very keen on devoting their one day of rest to possibly tiresome and cheerless worship, and being harangued by their 'betters'. They were keener than we are, certainly, but still not *that* keen. In any case, these 'amateur' clergymen often resorted to buying published books of sermons and reading them out in rotation, rather than share their own views or address the problems of their congregation. This meant that they did not spend hours agonisingly composing their own sermons of relevance to their flock. Nor did it galvanise the mildly faithful congregation to greater religious fervour, of course, since most of them probably could not understand why they, particularly, might be destined for eternal damnation, after their difficult life on earth, especially since the law seemed to be against them in so many ways. Being poor did not mean being stupid.

But, for the wealthier, this left a lot of time for other intellectual or philanthropic pursuits among those who wanted a purpose in life, rather than just 'playing' at being the rector or vicar. We owe a huge, if incidental, debt to the clergy with time on their hands. The roll-call of the clever clergy is staggering, and encompasses every aspect of learning, including much that you would not expect from men of the cloth. With time on their hands, education, income, and a great curiosity, many of them contributed to astronomy, physics, philosophy, mathematics, natural history – and the law, in a way that can only be described as lucky for us. One does suspect that some did not end their lives as wholehearted believers.

If the church or army did not appeal, there was always a career in the law. This was a favoured occupation for the sons of the gentry as it was a very useful background for property management or a political career. In fact, Parliament used to sit only from the afternoons onwards to allow MPs to pursue their legal careers in the morning. It has been estimated that by the end of the seventeenth century there were as many as 3,000 barristers in England and Wales, and possibly twice as many attorneys (solicitors). If true, this is fairly astonishing and attests to the litigious nature of the times. Sadly, being a man of the law did not preclude swindling and other illegal activities and the 'rogue' lawyer was a well-known phenomenon.

But to understand the effects of all this upon law and justice, it is necessary to travel further back in time, even to the Middle Ages.

The struggle for equality and democracy had continued over the centuries, of course, waxing and waning via many interesting and contradictory waymarks, as is usual for human endeavours. The ravages of the Black Death, for example, changed the balance of power between landowners and serfs when the former suddenly found themselves severely short of the previously-cowed workers to sustain their own estates and lifestyles. This led to some beneficial renegotiation of duties, rights, and remuneration.

The notion that a Parliament of the people, no matter how loosely 'democratic', should openly debate and make the laws of the land persisted, despite some monarchs fighting against it. Charles I paid for his obduracy and sense of entitlement with his life, despite reluctantly making several concessions to the principles of equality and the liberties of the people. He would insist that kings, like him, were divinely-appointed, which was a concept that did not endear itself to the Puritans, despite the fact that Oliver Cromwell himself believed he was divinely-ordained to lead the revolution. In fact, Cromwell, who rose to power as a liberator for the people, unsurprisingly proved to be autocratic in government and actually dithered for a while when it was suggested that he should become 'king'. The Commonwealth, under Cromwell, survived for just a few years before the Restoration of the monarchy under Charles II. Charles II was the complete antithesis of the bleak years of Puritanism, and contributed considerably to the merriment of the nation, even though he cost it a fortune in the process. But, maybe, freedom and fun is worth it. He certainly foreshadowed the Georgian sense of adventure.

Oddly, it was 'boring' Queen Anne, the forerunner of the Georgians and Charles II's niece, who really allowed the times to change. Doubtless preoccupied by her eighteen miscarriages and still-births, she had less time or instinct to enforce the privileges and power of the Crown. George I, the original Hanoverian, was a Protestant who spoke little English and who really just wanted to go home, but who ascended to the throne after her death via his descent from Elizabeth of Bohemia, the daughter of James I. The main virtue he possessed was that he was a Protestant, given the 1701 Act of Settlement, which prohibited a Catholic succession. The time was ripe for Parliamentary power to prevail, and for the modern Constitutional monarchy to begin to take some sort of shape. It is ironic that a queen charged mainly with producing a viable male heir, and a reluctant distant German kinsman when she couldn't, should have played such vital roles in promoting Parliament and democracy, in what would, after various Acts of Union, form first Great Britain, and then ultimately the United Kingdom of England, Scotland, Wales, and Northern Ireland.

By the eighteenth century, Parliament was sitting regularly and was very much in charge. It was, of course, largely composed of toffs, but not all of them were devoted to merely promoting their own interests.

The Statute of Anne 1710 (or Copyright Act) gave protection to authors for the first time. Prior to that anyone could plagiarise their work, and their status in the performing arts was generally somewhat lower than that of the theatre cat, whose role was to vanquish vermin.

Other legislation, however, had more far-reaching effects, although often not quite what the legislators had in mind. How one does relish the populist Law of Unintended Consequences.

The Marriage Act 1753, 'An Act for the Better Preventing of Clandestine Marriage', popularly known as Lord Hardwicke's Marriage Act, was the first statutory legislation in England and Wales to require a formal ceremony of marriage performed by an Anglican clergyman in accordance with canon law. This involved complex rules about the obtaining of a licence, parental consent, and the publication of banns. Until then, ordinary people occasionally just did not bother due to the expense, and common law acknowledged long-term partnerships anyway by way of cohabitation and repute. Indeed, unless one had a legacy to leave and the inheritance of the first-born son to consider, this could make sense, and people could make their own peace with God. However, the marital status of the poor was not Lord Hardwicke's concern. He was concerned with the ages of affluent or socially-important lovers, and the consent of their parents. As usual, the Law of Unintended Consequences struck and, after 1753, led to runaway marriages in Gretna Green and other towns just north of the border, since Scotland had different laws. Hardwicke's Act required parental consent if the parties were under 21-years old, but in Scotland it was vastly different. In Scotland boys aged 14, and girls aged 12, could get married without parental consent. This led to some forced marriages of abducted English heiresses, such as that of Edward Wakefield and the 15-year-old Ellen Turner, which was nullified by Parliament, with Robert Peel leading the charge in the House. By the nineteenth century, however, the Scots were somewhat alarmed, and had amended their laws to take account of age, and impose some (not very demanding) residency qualifications.

A visitor to Georgian England is hardly likely to fall foul of legal issues surrounding marriage or legacies, though. That would take time.

Rather more likely is becoming a debtor. Prisons were often places of incarceration for people who owed money to creditors, rather than ordinary felons, but could sometimes be rather relaxed institutions. In Georgian times, over half the prison population were deprived of their liberty to varying extents because of debt. If you either had connections or a means of earning money, you would merely be confined under fairly benign circumstances, with considerable leniency, until you had paid your creditors and sufficiently tipped the prison staff to gain your freedom. If you were poor, you might end up despairing your life away. The notorious Marshalsea prison in Southwark catered to both categories of debtor.

Oddly, there is an association between debtors and marriage. In eighteenth-century England, there was a surprising number of men of the church in debtors' prisons. In the Fleet prison, before the Marriage Act of 1753, it was commonplace for churchmen confined for debt to earn some money by marrying couples cheaply, and without asking any awkward questions. These were either 'irregular' or 'clandestine' marriages. Irregular marriages at least had a licence and the banns called, but took place away from the home parish due to a quirk in the law allowing this to take place in the Fleet prison environs. Clandestine marriages were somewhat murkier affairs, dependent upon secrecy for one reason or another. Most people doing this, however, just wanted to either marry quickly or save money, and it is known that in the 1740s it was a very regular occurrence. If contemporary lithograph prints are to be believed it was a very jolly occasion, with passing strangers and costermongers joining in, and everybody smiling and cheering. The prison warders took a cut of the proceeds, of course, and the local tavern-keepers were extremely keen to promote their own involvement, both as facilitators and caterers. So commonplace was this remarkable practice that in 1846 John Southerden Burn published a *History of the Fleet Marriages*. He tells us that a print depicting such an event included the following lines

> Scarce had the coach discharg'd its trusty fare
> But gaping crowds surround th' amorous pair.
> The busy plyers make a mighty stir,
> And whisp'ring cry, D'ye want the Parson, sir?
> Pray step this way – just to the Pen in Hand,
> The Doctor's ready there at your command;
> This way, (another cries) Sir I do declare,
> The true and ancient Register is here.

A visitor to Georgian London should certainly plan to witness this popular subversion of the law before the rather joyless-sounding Lord Hawkesbury put an end to it.

All prisons at the time were private enterprises, run for profit, and were basically an extortion racket so far as both the debtors and owners were concerned. If well-off enough to pay the prison fees, the 'prisoner' would be allowed visitors or even cohabitees, have access to food and alcohol, and be allowed out during the day to earn the money to pay the creditors and thus gain their freedom. In *The Expedition of Humphry Clinker* (1771), the wonderful writer Tobias Smollet (1721–1771) allows a prison warder at Newgate to give vent to his resentment that, due to the innocent Clinker's wildly evangelistic sermons, the food and drink revenues in the 'restaurant' had fallen disastrously because all the accused are in the chapel trying to save their souls.

Charles Dicken's father John, the alleged model for Mr Micawber in *David Copperfield*, spent three months in Marshalsea, being joined by his wife and children, until the death of his mother and her legacy allowed him to pay the debt of £40 to his baker. This seems a rather remarkable sum to owe to one's baker. The poorest, however, could expect starvation and dreadful physical abuse from cruel, illiterate, and poorly-paid wardens. A Parliamentary committee reported in 1729 that 300 inmates had starved to death within only three months, and that almost a dozen a day could perish in hot weather.

If, however, you commit an offence and cannot afford even a rogue lawyer to defend you, the penalty might be transportation. This was a very popular solution to the problem of trouble-makers who could not be either let off or hanged. Prior to the American War of Independence (1775–1783), that colony had been the favoured destination. During the war, and before Australia became a viable destination from 1787, another solution was needed. Prison hulks were moored on the Thames, and in other ports, and were far worse than being sent to Maryland and Virginia. These were mostly old unseaworthy naval ships and the conditions aboard were simply atrocious, with overcrowding among the shackled prisoners, dreadful food, hard labour, damp and chill, fatal communicable diseases, wound infections, and vermin running rife.

One did not have to do much to find oneself so sentenced or confined. Twenty-one year old Mary Springham was sentenced to seven years transportation in 1786 for stealing a snuffbox and about £186 at contemporary values (Old Bailey records). She never came home. In fact, she settled in Sydney Cove, married one William Hambly who was a carpenter's mate on a ship on the Australia run, and presumably her descendants live there to this day. That, at least, was a happy ending but, nonetheless, the time-traveller should beware because both the law and public opinion were capricious. In the early eighteenth century, highwaymen and robbers were sometimes seen as folk heroes. When Jack Sheppard was hanged in 1724, after escaping from prison four times, it is said that 200,000 people (mostly fans) attended his execution. This seems a somewhat remarkable estimate, and one struggles to imagine such a huge ghoulish crowd gathering around the gallows.

By the second half of the eighteenth century, however, ordinary people were taking a rather less accepting view of 'petty' criminals. The latter themselves had often previously displayed a rather insouciant attitude to their lifestyle choices and fate, and were prone to making jokes in court. Later Georgians, however, were rather more determined that the law should send a stronger message to miscreants.

This probably reflects the rise of the middle-classes, who now had assets and money to lose to crime, and growing political influence.

It is somewhat unlikely that the twenty-first century time-traveller to the eighteenth century would have any intention of breaking the law, but you never know. Misdemeanours to beware of committing include assault, which includes terrifying the victim by shouting and gestures; barratry, which was the offence of stirring up quarrels by spreading false rumours and prosecuting malicious lawsuits; libel, rioting, threatening behaviour, and vagabonding, which was begging under false pretences and often targeted gypsies. There were also various acts of Breaking the Peace. These included malicious damage to property, arson, and miscellaneous damage which included burning hayricks, killing farm animals, damaging trees, roots or plants, cutting down a riverbank, or destroying a fish pond. Industrial Revolution offences include vandalising a piece of clothing while it was being worn, vandalising or destroying silk in a loom, or damaging the tools for silk weaving (a statutory offence from 1766). Also proscribed were attempting to demolish a house (unless it was in a riot, when other penalties were incurred), and breaking and entering a non-dwelling house with intent to steal.

It is interesting to contemplate how many of these misdemeanours might impact on our modern on-line life, or result in much quieter weekends in town centres, if they were still rigorously-enforced. The offences of being drunk and disorderly, or incapable, were rather rare until the late eighteenth century, however, even though legislation existed to prosecute them. This was despite the Gin Craze, which struck the poor of London and provoked outrage and concern from the 1740s onwards. Gin was ludicrously cheap and not subject to quality controls or rules. For just a few pennies, people could find solace from their weary and unpleasant lives in the slums, companionship from like-minded boozers, and some (short-lived) fun. In 1730, it has been estimated that ten million gallons of gin were being distilled in the capital, and sold from seven thousand dram shops. Rudimentary statistics suggest that the average Londoner drank sixty-four litres of the dubious spirit a year. Since many people obviously did not, this means that some drank far more. For the first time, women were welcome in gin shops alongside men, which led to inevitable knock-on effects on family life, and the tag 'Mother's Ruin'.

Another trap for the unwary visitor might be offences against the king. This was not only the king, but his subjects as a nation, and included acts such as counterfeiting or interfering with the currency. So, if you are tempted to take along with you some fake Georgian money, then make sure it is foolproof.

Religion also fell into this category. Catholics were still persecuted, theoretically at least, until the Catholic Relief Acts in the nineteenth century. Needless to say, blasphemy was still an offence, which might cause a few problems for the outspoken modern sceptic. It was also an offence to pretend to have divine powers, so it would be highly unwise to claim to either speak to the dead or have supernatural knowledge of what the future might hold.

Under no circumstances criticise the monarch, whether in print or the spoken word. Plenty of people did of course, in this age of the lampoon, but they had some protection by being members of a metropolitan media elite which the authorities were reluctant to confront. You might well fall foul of seditious libel, seditious words, or seducing from allegiance, if not actual treason.

For the average, inquisitive and peaceable history buff however, law and order should not be a great problem, once adequately briefed.

Chapter Eight

A Night at the Opera

As with other aspects of Georgian life, the time traveller will find a surprisingly modern approach to going out, seeing people, and – very importantly – being seen. London was comparatively small then and, although all strata of society had their own places to go, they did mingle surprisingly often at public venues, if usually suitably segregated by both class and money. The eighteenth century saw the beginning of the media explosion with newspapers, magazines and advertising reaching the literate with information about people, events and opinion which led, perhaps unsurprisingly, to the birth of a celebrity culture. The Georgians were just as fascinated as we are by actors, singers, politicians, royalty and aristocrats and, having far less at home in the way of amusement, were very keen on going out to the theatre and the opera where such interesting people could be found. This was not only because it was fun, but because it also saved on home lighting and heating, with the former being particularly tedious depending, as it did, upon dim candles or lamps which always needed constant attention.

However, the twenty-first century visitor to the eighteenth century London theatre-land will find it a rather bewildering and, possibly, chaotic experience. The height of rudeness now is considered a failure to turn off one's mobile phone during the performance. The Georgians, had they had them, would have been cheerfully shrieking away and the play would have been drowned out by ringtones and cries of 'I'm at the theatre!'.

So, how to make the most of a rather startling visit to the theatre, opera, or other place of public performance, such as the pantomime or the circus?

If, before you visit the theatre, you did not manage to have dinner or, maybe, you tend to get peckish later, then you will be in good company. Picnics and drinking in the auditorium were commonplace. Nobody expected their whole attention to be focused on the entertainment, and were in the habit of setting up card tables in boxes, strolling around to greet their friends, gawping noisily at the famous, sharing food and drink, and generally socialising or networking. The wealthier and more nattily-dressed might even pay a premium to join in with the production by sitting on-stage and adding their own witticisms or improvements, to either the applause or derision of those in the audience who were actually paying attention. Theatres were lit by candle chandeliers and there was very little difference between the stage and auditorium lighting, thus failing to distinguish the performance from the audience. This may not seem such a vital distinction until one contemplates the hush that descends on the modern audience when the house lighting subsides and that on-stage springs into life. We go to the theatre to see the play and the actors, but the Georgians often went just to see each other.

The Georgian attention span at the theatre thus seems to have been somewhat short, and producers and actors did not generally seem to expect anything otherwise. Replete diners in private houses, quaffing a last brandy, might have earlier sent their footmen to occupy good seats so that they could turn up for the second half of the play to greet their friends, possibly knowing nothing whatsoever about the first half. Performances began early and the Georgians seemed to have had no concept of the queue, and nor were the seats numbered. This meant that from about an hour before the performance began there was a scrum to gain admittance, particularly for the cheaper seats in the top gallery (the Gods) or the pit, which was standing only. Injury, or even death, was not an unknown occurrence during the melee. The truly grand patrons were subscribers of course, who had a box reserved for them from which they could overlook the stage and gaze down at the less fortunate in the audience. Boxes also had a private room behind them, as they often still do today, in which patrons could entertain their guests or consort with ladies of dubious virtue.

Prices were reduced after the first half in order to fill the Gods with servants or the general hoi polloi. One supposes that a keen servant might actually have known far more about the play if he habitually occupied his master's good seat for the first half, and then retreated to the Gods for the second half. If he could hear what was going on, of course. During the Victorian nineteenth century, the unruly behaviour of the theatregoers was eventually harnessed to some sort of order, thanks to the advent of limelight and the determination that any audience participation should be either organised and controlled, or supressed – usually in the name of a polite social or educational benefit or, indeed, because people just preferred to know what was going on, and get some value for their money. Georgian theatre-goers did have a certain respect for classical drama, like Shakespeare, but also very much enjoyed fun being poked at their betters and rulers.

The enthusiasm for satire of both writers and their audiences was a grave problem, to the mind of eighteenth-century governments. People in theatres – playwrights, actors and theatre-goers – were saying very rude things indeed about their betters and rulers, and to the considerable merriment and disdain of the nation. The eighteenth century saw an explosion of public satire and mild social rebellion but this, of course, was not new, as people have poked fun at their masters for millennia. Some of them had to be very brave, or angry, to do this as the personal consequences could be dire. This was not the case in Georgian England, however. One gets the impression that the mighty were fighting a rather rear-guard action against such public scoffing. The media, the theatre and the publishing industry gave voice and reach to many iconoclasts – including Swift, Hogarth, Gillray, Rowlandson, Sheridan, and that apparent pillar of the Establishment, Henry Fielding, who managed to be both a satirist and a magistrate. The French writer, Voltaire, took refuge from the French *Ancien Régime* in London between 1726–1729, having been persecuted and imprisoned in his own country for his unorthodox views, and he loved us. Arriving penniless and allegedly with hardly a word of English, inside three years he had learned enough to understand and appreciate Shakespeare, Swift, and a culture which allowed citizens to say what they thought:

> 'How I love the English boldness!' Voltaire said. 'How I love those who say what they think! ... It is a treasure house of jokes, of which the rest of the world has no idea. Pascal only makes jokes at the expense of the Jesuits, but Swift entertains and instructs us at the expense of the whole human race.'

One can infer from these remarks, perhaps, that Voltaire remained, at heart, a true Frenchman in that he conflated France with the rest of the world. In the Germanic states, however, a suitably intellectual and rather ponderous academic argument discussed the use of satire to promote morality; the Italians were certainly fond of poking fun at the lofty and self-important; and the Jews have always been renowned for a spiky and well-directed sense of humour. But it may have been true that none were quite so devoted to the art of jeering at the mighty as were the trenchantly-disrespectful British, who had staggered through murderous monarchs, religious strife and Puritanism, civil war, the Glorious Revolution that peacefully brought William and Mary to the throne, and still somehow come out the other side with their iconoclasm and humour intact.

What was newer, however, was that the British Enlightenment culture did not see fit to imprison or, worse, execute such outspoken nuisances, as might have been the fate of political or artistic dissidents in earlier centuries. The emerging Enlightenment society prided itself on being rational and democratic, and given to balanced scientific and philosophical argument, as outwardly reflected in its devotion to Georgian neo-classical architecture. A different political solution was needed rather than brute suppression by force.

In 1737 the government, or more probably the first 'Prime Minister' Robert Walpole, decided that the answer to such public impudence was benign censorship, and declared that all theatres must be licensed, and plays submitted for approval before staging. The final straw was, apparently, a play called *The Golden Rump* which made scatological suggestions about King George II and his queen, but many suspected that it was his own authority being undermined that really bothered Walpole. He had been mercilessly lampooned by John Gay in the highly popular *Beggar's Opera*, which had compared him to an underworld overlord, and he had had enough. In fact, *The Golden Rump* was never performed on stage, was only ever quoted in the House of Commons, and – in the absence of a verifiable author – was suspected of being either the work of the unreliable Henry Fielding, or written at the behest of Walpole himself (in order to enable the censorship law). This Act, of course, was the beginning of over 200 years of censorship under the auspices of the Lord Chamberlain's Office until, in 1968, it was decided that the public were not children and, possibly, that artistic freedom and satire were an essential part of a culture which prided itself on democracy and freedom of speech. Besides, with a television in every house, and young writers and performers pushing at every boundary, it was not working anyway.

The result of this Act was that, for a long while during the eighteenth century, only two theatres in London were granted a licence – Covent Garden, and the Theatre Royal in Drury Lane, and very grand they became as a result. The brand 'Theatre Royal' became a shorthand for a licensed venue, and was exported from London to the provinces, as can still be seen today in many places such as Nottingham, Plymouth, Windsor, Brighton, and so many others. Unlicensed theatres described themselves as 'playhouses' and widely populated the rest of the country, and rather more successfully.

These other, unlicensed, venues were obliged to find a way around the constraints of the law which, of course, they promptly did. A brief perusal of the 1737 Act revealed that only *complete* plays were to be submitted for approval to the Lord Chamberlain, but not short playlets, or music. So was born the entertainment which eventually became variety theatre, featuring singers, acrobats, jugglers, burlesque dancers – with the satirical or otherwise naughty sketches sandwiched between the other acts and, thus, safely away from the Lord Chamberlain's reproving scrutiny.

Samuel Johnson who, like every member of the public was not allowed to listen to Parliamentary debate in person, relied upon second-hand accounts from MP friends and general gossip to generate 'fictional' articles for our old acquaintance, *The Gentleman's Magazine*, and is said by some to be the original sketch writer, and a source of inspiration for the performers in the playhouses. The Lord Chamberlain was not even entirely successful at censoring plays, however, and quite a few jokes were smuggled past him and his officials to the glee of their rather more streetwise audiences. In fact, the scurrilous lampooning of political and high society figures reached its zenith after 1780 and only subsided somewhat after the 1820s. Much of this was actually in the form of caricature by artists and cartoonists, possibly because they were further ahead of the game than writers when it came to appreciating that 'brevity is the soul of wit' – as rather ironically asserted by the verbose Polonius in Shakespeare's *Hamlet*.

But what of the writers and performers themselves?

Up until the mid-eighteenth century 'acting' was a curiously stilted business, and it took the famous actor-manager, David Garrick (1717–1779), to bring about a gradual change to a more naturalistic approach to drama and story-telling. Until his directorship, actors stood still and struck a dramatic pose to declaim their lines in a very loud voice, which was probably the only way to get anyone's attention given the amiable chaos in the auditorium. Clasping a hand to the bosom or brow, or pointing, were common dramatic devices. One does wonder if Shakespeare had in mind such performances when he interspersed his dramatic scenes with so-called comedy as a form of more naturalistic light relief or, more subtly, a subversive and satirical potential. In Shakespeare's plays, clowns and jesters pop up everywhere and, often, in the least likely of places, such as in *King Lear* and *Hamlet*. They have an artistic licence to freely speak the truth, craftily humiliate their masters and get away with it, or at least present a different viewpoint which is denied to the serious characters. The possibilities of such an artistic device were not lost on eighteenth century writers and cartoonists, who were happy to cast ordinary and poorer citizens in the role of either wise fools or naive dupes, to counterpoint the wickedness or venality of their so-called betters. Robert Walpole, and other dignitaries, did not much like such disrespectfulness.

The elevation of Shakespeare to The Bard, and national treasure, began in the eighteenth century. He already had, of course, a considerable reputation which made it quite difficult for the Lord Chamberlain to veto any aspect of a performance. Georgian producers, however, were not always satisfied with the Bard's denouments, or even, indeed, his prose and poetry. A happy ending, they often decided, sent the audience home feeling good and more likely to return to spend even more money at the theatre in future. They also preferred rhyme to blank verse. Eighteenth-century re-interpretations of Shakespeare included changing words so that his poetry rhymed, chopping out 'boring' sections or characters, re-writing his (certainly not always accurate) history, and converting tragedies into less frankly stark tear-jerkers – such as allowing Romeo and Juliet a final consoling conversation in the tomb, which they never had. In defence of these eighteenth-century Bard-tinkerers one should perhaps take account of the intellectual demands Shakespeare places upon his audiences, which one can see might have been a bit difficult given the habits and behaviour of Georgian theatre-goers. Another reason may be that by the eighteenth century, the English language had already evolved quite a long way towards modern vocabulary and syntax. The twenty-first century audience will generally find it much easier to instinctively grasp a Sheridan play, for example, or to read Swift, than to understand Shakespeare without already knowing the plot and characters, and it is entirely possible that the Georgians felt their own attention and reverence waning somewhat without the 'improvements'.

This brings us back to the giant of the eighteenth-century theatre, David Garrick, who was largely responsible for the establishment of Shakespeare as the greatest writer in the English language. He did not much approve of the 'improvements' that other producers inflicted upon both the plots and poetry, although it has to be admitted that he did indulge in a spot of tinkering himself, albeit in somewhat less disastrous ways. He reduced *Hamlet* from over four hours to about three and, having once restively sat through the uncut version, I can only applaud his decision.

Whatever tinkering he did undertake, however, is less notable than his insight that acting should be just that – *acting* and, therefore, as naturalistic and realistic as possible. If we were to attend one of his productions we might not agree these days, used as we are to close camera work and good theatre acoustics. He was criticized for overt gestures and gurning by some, but compared to the bombastic theatrical declamations which had preceded him, his productions were a revelation which enraptured the Georgian theatre-going public. In fact, his celebrity contributed to the founding of 'spouting clubs' to mimic Garrick and other famous actors and actresses. They met in taverns and amateur theatres to act out scenes and speeches that they had either seen or read. Considerable academic effort has been expended on wondering why they did this and learned conclusions have been reached concerning 'cultural convergence', which re-confirmed celebrity status. I think, though, that they were merely having rather wistful fun, just as we do with karaoke and tribute bands.

Garrick also took it upon himself to improve the behaviour of the audiences, which cannot have been easy, and paved the way for the more decorous behaviour we have exhibited at the theatre ever since the Victorians. Garrick, of course, was a theatrical Titan, but there were plenty of others treading the boards who fuelled the Georgian fascination with thespians.

For women, a career on the eighteenth-century stage was considered somewhat unusual, and, no matter how appealing they were to their public then, they are now chiefly suspected of being titillatingly immoral for their times. The Georgians, captivated by the glamour of these ladies, may not in fact have felt quite that way or, indeed, have decided that it did not matter very much. In previous centuries, decent women did not go on the stage and female parts were played by boys, dressed as girls, and piping away in an unconvincing treble. We, of course, would feel deeply uncomfortable if confronted by a pre-pubescent boy playing a love scene with a grown man, but audiences before the seventeenth century felt differently. By the eighteenth century, however, this had changed and the novelty of women on stage entranced their audiences, rather to the annoyance of David Garrick who sometimes exhibited a somewhat churlish jealousy towards his increasingly-popular leading ladies. The most famous forerunner of the eighteenth-century actresses was, of course, Nell Gwyn, the much beloved mistress of Charles II in the previous century. This feisty and funny lady overcame the rumours and disapproval of her previous lifestyle by being talented, clever, and compassionate. She was philanthropic and benevolent, and people appreciated that, particularly given her humble beginnings and, when she died at only 37, she left a legacy to Newgate prisoners.

Nell was a great character, who captured the heart of a king, and even eventually managed to have amicable tea parties with her great rival for the king's affections, the very aristocratic Louise de Kerouaille, the Duchess of Portsmouth. No doubt they were doing what all men most dread amongst their women-folk; making friends with each other – and swapping anecdotes and observations.

The louche reputation of actresses was probably the greatest intrigue for aristocratic and wealthy young men, buzzing around the capital's many social attractions, in defiance of their parents' appalled better judgement. After all, before you inevitably settled down with the young lady of your parents' choice, who was virtuous, inexperienced and moneyed, you could maybe have some fun? Not even royalty was immune as can be judged from the long-lasting attachment of King George III's son, the Duke of Clarence and later King William IV, to the Anglo-Irish actress, Dorothea Jordan. The Prince Regent, later George IV, also included at least two actresses among his many mistresses.

Most of us know that, in the nineteenth and early twentieth centuries, young men married 'unsuitable' women, from actresses to rich Americans, and from chorus girls to even the daughters of wealthy criminals. One reason for this was the inheritance tax, introduced by Lloyd George in 1909 which made life very difficult indeed for the aristocracy. Firstly, this made for the irresistible exchange of new money for an old aristocratic title and, secondly, there was the often deplored, but frequently successful, freedom of younger sons to marry someone who looked like being rather more fun than a bishop's dutiful daughter. But this social tendency does predate the inheritance tax, and no doubt contributed to a considerable diaspora of wealth and genes from which many people might have actually benefited over the last 250 years. One explanation for this was possibly the lure of the capital, London; its temptations, and its undoubted expenses. The litany of aristocratic scions marrying 'unsuitable' women is quite remarkable, especially from the performing arts professions. And that is without otherwise (few, but often very high-profile) suitable brides from the upper classes eventually proving themselves to be quite the opposite, as they too were sometimes rather more attracted to actors and performers than to their dull or unfaithful husbands.

Gossip from the eighteenth century regarding the three aristocratic Lennox sisters, the great-granddaughters of Charles II and his mistress Louise claims that these women, among many others, all went somewhat wrong in the marital stakes despite the fact that they were socially accepted and valued. Given their ancestors, that might not be too surprising. Their own father married at 18 and abandoned his wife to go on the Grand Tour. Returning three years later, it is said that he visited the theatre only to be startled by a lovely woman whom he did not recognise, in a box, surrounded by admirers. It was his own wife. Good gracious!

One problem with Georgian theatres was their tendency to catch fire and kill the patrons. By our standards the Georgians were not overly concerned with Health & Safety issues, possibly because life in general was fraught with hazard and the notion of risk assessment might have seemed rather daunting, or even bizarre. It is also true that the solutions to a lot of their problems awaited developments in science and technology which, although nascent in the eighteenth century, were still distant by a century or so for practical purposes. One hazard which did concern them, however, was the danger of fire at theatres. Public and domestic lighting was still dependent upon naked flames, whether candles or lamps. The latter, of course, had a measure of safety built into them, shielded as they were with a glass flue, but they relied upon oil and a lot of tedious wick-trimming and other maintenance, which had to be carried out every half hour or so to keep them working efficiently, so were hardly suitable for lofty chandeliers in public places, like theatres. Cooking and heating were dependent upon labour-intensive solid-fuel stoves and hearths, and it is small wonder that many women, in long, swirling and combustible clothing, met with horrible accidents in the home.

In the public arena, theatres were particularly vulnerable to the risk of fire and this helped to bring about the beginnings of legislation to make buildings safer. In 1774 the Fires Prevention (Metropolis) Act was passed into law which was mainly aimed at confining a fire to the area in which it began, and stopping its spread rather than preventing it in the first place, which was sensible enough given the ubiquity of naked flames.

One of the most famous episodes of a theatrical conflagration was, of course, Shakespeare's Globe which caught fire in 1613 due to the fact that a real cannon, loaded with gunpowder and wadding, was fired in the interests of verisimilitude at a performance of *Henry VIII*. The resulting sparks set fire to the thatched roof which collapsed, and the wooden stands began to burn

merrily. Remarkably, nobody was badly hurt, and the only recorded incident
is one of a man's trousers catching fire, and he was saved by a friend who
threw his beer over the smouldering garment. Moving forward 100 years or so
however, and there were far more public entertainments at which hundreds of
people were corralled in buildings with many possible sources of conflagration,
only one or two exits, no fire brigade, and no evacuation procedures to stem
the inevitable panic should the worst occur. The exteriors of such theatres
might have been of stone or brick, but the interiors were of wood, and were lit
by devices employing mostly naked flames. Somewhat alarmed after previous
incidents the re-built (after a fire) Drury Lane theatre introduced, in 1794,
an iron safety curtain which could be lowered to separate the audience from
the stage. Somewhat counter-intuitively, given the legendary bad behaviour
of audiences, this was to protect them against dangerous props, ill-advised
theatrical ruses, and the consequent risk of fire. The theatre also had a large
water tank on the roof to douse any conflagration, although we do not know
if it would have worked or, indeed, how. Science was also wading into the
problem, insisting as it did that chemical fire-proofing was possible when it
came to props and scenery, which was true. Today, we are mostly grateful for
Health & Safety legislation, even if it is sometimes annoying and obstructive.
In the Georgian era it was a comparatively new concept, which often cost
money to implement, and circumscribed freedom.

A visit to the opera, however, might be a slightly less unruly experience. In
England it has always been an upper-class diversion for the more mature and
sedate. The sheer volume of an orchestra, chorus, and leading singers with huge
lungs, possibly curtailed the more exuberant behaviour associated with plays.
Most of Europe (except the French) was in thrall, perhaps understandably, to
lovely Italian opera. The Italians themselves, however, were behaving rather like
our own play-goers. Hector Berlioz, the great composer, went to hear *L'Elisir
d'Amore* at La Scala in the early nineteenth century and reported in disgust:

People were talking in normal voices with their backs to the stage.
The singers, undeterred, gesticulated and yelled their lungs out in the
strictest spirit of rivalry. At least I presumed they did from their wide-
open mouths, but the noise of the audience was such that no sound
penetrated except the bass drum. People were gambling, eating supper
in their boxes etc., etc. Consequently, perceiving it was useless to expect
to hear anything of the score, which was then new to me, I left.

Furthermore, an English visitor to La Scala remarked about the boxes which 'catered' to the better-off, that sometimes the curtains of the boxes were drawn during performances, 'and you may imagine what you please'.

The English, however, true to an island race with an agenda of their own, were experimenting with opera written in their own tongue, beginning in the seventeenth century with Henry Purcell. He is best known for *Dido & Aeneas*, but he died aged only thirty-six in 1695. After his death, interest in opera sagged somewhat until the 1730s when the giants Thomas Arne and George Frederic Handel rose to fame. Arne had little success initially with his unfortunately-named *The Temple of Dullness* (1745), but triumphed later with *Thomas & Sally* and *Artaxerxes* in the 1770s. It is certain that a night at the opera in eighteenth-century England might not be quite the reverent experience we now expect when spending a small fortune to attend Covent Garden or the Coliseum, but nonetheless there are fewer reports of people behaving appallingly.

In the eighteenth century, however, London or other Royal Theatre venues were not where most people went for entertainment, and the venturesome time-traveller should follow suit. Quite apart from the less-regulated playhouses, there was the circus. For this entertainment we have to thank one Philip Astley (1742–1814), an ex-soldier with a great talent for trick riding. As one might expect, he did not conceive the whole travelling-circus concept we now understand, but he did put in place the idea that a circular arena for performances involving horses and riders would be better for the spectators at his riding school (opened 1770), Astley's Amphitheatre. He also subsequently realised that other amusements, in between the acts of dashing horses and acrobatic riders, might be a profitable idea. Bring on the clowns – and jugglers, music, dancing dogs and, eventually, more exotic animals. Astley ran his serious riding school in the mornings, and devoted the afternoons to spectacle.

Clowns, somewhat sinister characters, who are now dignified with their own noun referring to a fear of them – coulrophobia – did not originate in England, and seem to have a history going back to the ancient Egyptians. Until the advent of the circus, clowns were not intended to amuse children and, indeed, most of us probably have memories of uneasy encounters with them when very young. In fact, clowns are reputed to have a deeply disturbing history involving murder, depression, alcoholism, financial ruin, paedophilia, and infidelity. It must be admitted, though, that probably any occupation would also be similarly culpable if it were subject to scrutiny – including monarchs, lawyers, doctors, politicians, priests, actors etc.

Pantomime was also evolving in the eighteenth century, being a curiously English amalgam of music, satire, and the (originally Italian) characters of Harlequin and Columbine from the *Commedia Dell'Arte*. At the beginning, mime was the main theme, but this did not capture the English audience. Given behaviour at events where people were loudly declaiming or singing, one can hardly imagine that silent mime would succeed in capturing the audiences' attention. Ultimately, song and dance became particularly important in this very popular entertainment as the eighteenth century progressed, as was the element of slapstick. Even David Garrick felt he should stage his own panto, but decided that Harlequin should speak instead of miming, thus mercifully rescuing us from an enduring British version of Marcel Marceau.

The Georgians were considerably more robust than we are when it came to the elision of violence and humour, so the twenty-first century visitor must be prepared to be rather shocked when visiting places of public entertainment. People (not all, of course) who found amusement in public executions, animal-baiting, mental health issues, brutal fighting, and the vicissitudes of extreme poverty, can scarcely be thought to be compassionate in any modern social sense. But they lived their lives on the edge of both an authoritarian Cromwellian legacy and an Enlightenment future, with both religion and natural philosophy confusing their attitudes and behaviour. In the eighteenth century, people either swam or sank beneath the waves of change. Those who swam adapted to social, political and economic change, and many of the wealthier contributed either financially or philosophically to the philanthropy which is now mostly attributed to the emerging Victorian social conscience. But most people were both habituated to, and liked, the sort of public 'fun' we would deplore.

Perhaps the last tale of late Georgian theatre should be devoted to Mr Robert 'Romeo', 'Diamond' or 'Curricle' Coates, a wealthy amateur of the stage, who was born in Antigua in 1772 and first seems to have come to the attention of English audiences in 1809, at Bath, in the reign of King George IV. He was a late eighteenth-century Georgian, and bore the thespian legacy of the times. His sad story is set at the opposite end of the spectrum of acting ability to the mighty David Garrick and considers a strange and pathetic, but kind and gentle man, who wanted to be an actor, who had no talent whatsoever, but who was *so* bad ... he was good. At least, from the point of view of the cruel audiences, who were only after an evening's entertainment of any sort. Including human bear-baiting.

Mr Coates particularly believed that his talents lay in interpreting the classics, which is why one of his soubriquets was 'Romeo'. The other two celebrated his preferred mode of transport (the curricle) and his penchant for personal and dazzling bling (diamonds). He first began acting in his native Antigua as a very young man, and at a time when the West Indies had very little in the way of social entertainment, so his lack of talent was ignored as the islanders were inclined to accept anything they could get. This, however, was no preparation for the reception the English gave his performances a few years later. A Mr Pryse Gordon says, in his memoirs, that he first encountered Mr Coates when they shared lodgings in Bath and he was startled to note that the latter loudly and dramatically rehearsed passages from Shakespeare over breakfast. Mr Pryse Gordon found this 'fairly striking' and, although he was impressed by the verve of the performance, couldn't help but comment that Mr Coates departed somewhat from the text. Mr Coates serenely replied that he knew the original text by heart, but thought he had improved upon it. This, as we know of course, was not particularly unusual, so one can perhaps understand Mr Pryse Gordon using his connections to promote an 1810 performance of *Romeo and Juliet* in Bath featuring Mr Coates. I remain rather suspicious about his motives. On that occasion, nothing worse than orange peel was thrown by the outraged theatre-goers, and the curtain did not fall until Act V when Romeo seized a crowbar to break into Juliet's tomb. The audience then became seriously restive, and the rest of the performance had to be abandoned. Mr Coates' biographers noted that he appeared as Romeo in a cloak of sky blue, crimson pantaloons, a huge white hat trimmed with feathers, and that the whole ensemble sparkled with diamonds.

Mr Coates was not deterred from his thespian ambitions by this less than rapturous reception. Far worse was to happen, however, when he transferred his performances to London, after farcical goings-on at Brighton and Cheltenham. Things rapidly got out of hand, and not only was the health and safety of Mr Coates threatened, but also that of his fellow-actors. A performance at Richmond prior to his West End debut ended when some young men in the audience laughed so hard that medical attention had to be sought, and they were carried outside to recover. Mr Coates was annoyed at this flagrant disregard of his efforts and castigated the (absent) culprits by allegedly extemporising from the footlights:

> Ye Bucks of the boxes there, who roar and reel,
> Too drunk to listen and too proud to feel.
> Whose flinty hearts are proof against despair,
> Whose vast estates are neither here nor there

One can understand how upset he felt. He was making valid points, despite the fact that he was the cause of it all, but he does seem to have been prepared with a speech. He was applauded by a small section of the audience who obviously had rather more empathy than most of the others.

Events began to move towards even more chaos, however, when Mr Coates appeared at the Haymarket theatre in 1811, in a production of Rowe's tragedy, *The Fair Penitent*, in the role of Lothario. One does wonder why that innocent and faithful husband, Mr Coates, ever thought he was suited to this challenge. It was a theatrical tragedy which turned into sheer farce, and riots ensued. Theatre-goers, during the play's short run, could never be sure if the performance would have to be brought to an abrupt end by the shrieking, whistling, cat-calls and threat to life and limb; or whether it would stagger to its conclusion when the 'Gifted Amateur', clad in astoundingly gaudy finery and many diamonds, would stage the death scene. What particularly delighted or enraged the audience was Lothario's habit, when collapsing to his demise, of spreading a handkerchief on the stage and carefully depositing his elaborate Spanish hat on it before assuming a dramatic death pose. On one occasion the hooting audience insisted this scene be reprised three times, which poor Mr Coates naively seems to have found flattering.

Sir Ian McKellen, among our twenty-first century thespians, can convince us of almost anything, however unlikely, but then he is a brilliant and professional actor with decades of training and experience. The intrepid Mr Coates, sadly, was not. But, by this time in his theatrical career, rumour had spread far and wide about the fun to be had by going to see him, and it was not a kindly recommendation. It is said that at least 1,000 people were turned away from the Haymarket theatre, and others offered as much as £5 to be admitted behind the stage. Among the horrible audience were dukes, earls, ambassadors and Knights of the Realm. Mr Coates, however, merely thought these luminaries were there because he was such a good actor. He had no idea. The torments visited upon this harmless and kindly man were truly terrible. After the Prince Regent had attended a performance, which Mr Coates ecstatically thought to be the pinnacle of social approval, he received an invitation to attend a royal ball and supper at Carlton House, the Regent's residence. One can only imagine the excitement and pride he felt, and he immediately ordered a new suit of unparalleled magnificence to be made for the event. He arrived in a chaise and waved graciously to the crowd that always gathered on such occasions to gawp, his diamonds flashing in the brilliant lighting. On presenting his invitation, however, he was told that it was a forgery and he was obliged to leave, passing those same now-derisive crowds, and return to his lodgings alone and without the long-departed chaise, humiliated, and in agonies of misery.

This is but a short account of the cruel humiliations visited upon this poor man, who never gave up his theatrical ambition. As an elderly man more shame was in store, however. His income from the West Indies evaporated, no doubt exacerbated by his personal extravagances and penchant for diamonds, and he owed money. He died at the age of seventy-seven, run over in Russell Street – by a curricle. His younger widow re-married almost immediately. But then, in those days, how else could a woman without means survive?

Chapter Nine

Gambling

The time traveller who fancies a flutter will find the vice well catered for in the eighteenth century, because the Georgians loved to gamble upon just about anything – from random events, to games of skill with rules, to unruly sports, and to bloodthirsty animal, or human, fights. All this, despite the fact that gaming was (theoretically) illegal outside members-only clubs and racecourses.

Gambling is predicated on balancing risks versus rewards, and the Georgians were certainly risk-takers. This is possibly because life itself was much riskier than we are prepared to tolerate on a day-to-day basis, given their shorter life-expectancy, child mortality, no welfare safety net, largely ineffectual (and frankly grim) medicine, and only a rather rudimentary governmental nod towards the notion of Health & Safety. Alongside this, however, was the doubtless intoxicating sense that the world was theirs for the grasping; they were building an Empire, and opportunity abounded. It is not surprising, then, that such a combination encouraged scientific, intellectual, economic, and business risk-taking. And gambling.

Even so, fears about the dire effects of gambling grew throughout the eighteenth century (along with its popularity) until, in 1784, a pamphlet published by an MP it is claimed, exhorted even more legislation and action. The writer reached rather wildly for support for his thesis that it would be the downfall of the Nation: 'To this dreadful vice must the loss of America be ascribed! To this dreadful vice must every misfortune which has lately fallen on this country be attributed!'

However, one must not ascribe addiction to this vice simply to British Georgians. Throughout recorded history there are dismal tales of gambling and its sorry consequences. Indeed, it is impossible to find a civilisation across the globe in which it was not a regular part of life for millennia, from Europe to Africa to the Middle and Far East and beyond, through the Pacific and to the New World. Dice, in their various forms, were ubiquitous, and stakes often included children, wives, and even mothers in some societies.

Among notable European gamblers can be found Cato, Casanova, Descartes, Montaigne, Oliver Goldsmith, Talleyrand, the lords Halifax, Byron and Shaftesbury, Beau Brummel, William Pitt – and those are only a few of the people about whom comment was thought worthy due to either their celebrity or stupendous losses.

Modern gaming (betting on chance) is usually a highly organised and corporate business, and even those who participate in casino games and machines, haunt the betting shops and on-line sites, or play the Lottery know – in their heart of hearts – that they are going to lose in the long run, because the odds are carefully, statistically and legally, stacked against them. This does not stop millions of people around the world from having an occasional or even habitual punt, of course, since the human spirit seems hard-wired to value hope over experience. This tendency probably served us well in evolutionary terms thousands of years ago, when our ancestors gazed at a distant mountain range and wondered optimistically if life would be better on the other side of it. This sort of exciting speculation is largely denied to us now, of course, so it is possible that we sublimate our longing for a better future into buying a weekly lottery ticket for a randomly-decided enterprise which offers absurd winnings for gambling on the even more absurd jackpot odds of about 45 million to one against.

> A Lottery is a taxation
> Upon all the fools in creation;
> And Heav'n be prais'd
> It is easily rais'd. . .
>
> Henry Fielding *The Lottery* (1731)

Indeed, one cannot help but wonder if even our distant ancestors gathered around the fire after a hard day's hunting and gathering, and gambled for choice morsels of food on the outcome of a human wrestling match, or on which of two beetles won a race.

The 'modern' state lottery was invented in the seventeenth century and for exactly the same reasons as ours; as a way of raising money for public projects whilst offering participants the chance of unearned life-changing riches. Previously, the Crown had intermittently resorted to lotteries as part of haphazard money-raising schemes, but the late seventeenth century State Lottery Acts were part of the financial innovations of the 1690s that established the Bank of England and the Stock Exchange. National lotteries underwrote state loans, reduced the capital or interest on the government debt, funded public projects, and raised revenue directly. They were thus lent a veneer of respectability and the possibility of success which seduced the public into 'investing'. It has often been observed that speculating on the Stock Exchange is little different to betting on horses, for example, and indeed lottery tickets were sold by brokers alongside stocks in Exchange Alley in London. The seventeenth and eighteenth centuries were the setting for some notable market crashes, including Tulip Mania (the 1630s) and the South Sea Bubble (1720), but stock dealings were only for the very few, unlike lotteries. The East India Company, for example, paid gratifyingly huge and tax-free dividends to fewer than 500 investors.

However, there were distinct differences between the early lotteries and ours today. Early lotteries were fundamentally a long-term loan to the government, so no investor actually lost out, although the government sometimes did. There was an assured return in an annuity, as well as the possibility of a large win in government bonds, and a guarantee of ultimate repayment with interest, so it may have been more like our Premium Bonds. But by 1769 the element of gambling had been established and every lottery contained blanks. It was possible to insure against the blanks with a company of some probity or, alternatively, one could resort to an unofficial 'Moroccan', who were somewhat seedy upholders of private enterprise who would insure a ticket for a fee which went straight into the red Moroccan wallets they carried.

The state lottery of 1693 heralded over 120 lotteries held during the next 130 years, and during the eighteenth century Britain went to war on loans raised by lotteries. They provided a third of Marlborough's campaign expenses, 40 per cent of what was spent trying to defend the American colonies, and more than a quarter of that used against fighting Napoleon. Less bellicose public projects included the building of Westminster Bridge and the British Museum at Montagu House.

The lottery in the eighteenth century was, therefore, different to its modern descendant in both its customer base and winning potential, and it also took place far less frequently which made it a considerable event. In fact, the emphasis on important and named public projects, the aspect of 'investment' and the State backing, ensured that it probably appealed very much to the burgeoning, wealthy, and aspirational middle classes, including merchants and bankers. The aristocracy, of course, was well used to being coerced into supporting the Crown and its ambitions, so they were less likely to be attracted. The poor could not afford a whole £10 ticket, but used to hopefully buy shares in a ticket (often as small as 1/64th), and were then inclined to buy the 'insurance' which led to some agitation among the great and the good. In 1787 there was a series of Parliamentary debates on the vexed topic of the lottery and insurance, with one MP even claiming that his own family was being financially hit by the consequences of the habit. One suspects that while he was sombrely doing his duty in Parliament, his relatives were enjoying very different pastimes.

By our standards, the eighteenth century lottery design was slightly more complicated, since we are used to ambling into a shop and just buying some numbers randomly generated by the till. The draw took place in public, most probably to reassure everyone that it was not rigged, rather than as a spectacle of entertainment, and was a lengthy process taking days. Needless to say, confidence in the probity of the lotteries was somewhat misplaced, despite the public draws, as abuse and fraud were common enough, and many people considered them a moral danger to society.

The Act to build a Westminster bridge from New Palace Yard to the opposite Surrey shore received the Royal Assent in 1736 and agreed that compensation should be paid to the ferrymen who would be put out of business. One of these was the Archbishop of Canterbury under whose auspices the Lambeth horse ferry operated. The usual methods of funding, such as private enterprise and tolls, were eschewed in favour of a lottery which led Sir Henry Fielding to call Westminster Bridge the 'bridge of fools', an epithet which stuck since it took fourteen years from the Act to its completion. The resulting beautiful bridge was painted by Canaletto and Turner, among others, but its lifespan was only from 1750 to 1862 because it was sinking into the clay due to weak foundations. The Victorians built our present bridge, having finally decided that the safety issues and cost of constant repairs could no longer be ignored. By this time, of course, Victorian morés were firmly against encouraging public gambling, even for good causes, so there was no immoral lottery involved.

The British Museum's remit, which was to be for the 'Use and Benefit of the Publick', was a direct result of the decision to fund it through a lottery. Previously, collections and libraries were only for the use of a very small and educated elite, and the notion that the general public might like to see and appreciate examples of mankind's artistic, scientific and literary heritage was considered, frankly, bizarre. But this elitism could hardly be sustained when the public were being asked to fund it. Besides, in the Age of Enlightenment, there was a growing belief among some philosophers, scientists and politicians, that improving education would be of both a moral and economic benefit for a country bent on expansionism, wealth and power.

Most eighteenth-century gambling was of a more social, and often venal, nature than the lotteries, however. And where better to start than at the very top of society, with a visit to White's, the archetypal London gentlemen's club, patronised by royalty and the aristocracy, as well as a few of the less socially-favoured but sufficiently wealthy and upwardly-mobile arrivistes from the upper middle classes. The club was notorious for gambling; its patrons were known as the 'gamesters of White's', and it was the source of the hellish decline of the Rake in Hogarth's *The Rake's Progress*. Jonathan Swift described it as 'the bane of half the English nobility'. One can only guess at how the princesses and peeresses felt about it, especially as women were banned.

White's began as first a chocolate, and then a coffee house in Mayfair, established in the seventeenth century by an Italian, Francesco Bianco (Francis White). Even then the Italians knew all about coffee. By the eighteenth century it was the haunt of the wealthy and powerful, and relocated to suitably grandiose premises in St James'. Notable members over the last 200 years have included Beau Brummel, Horace Walpole, Oswald Mosley, Evelyn Waugh, Lord Lucan, every prime minister between Robert Walpole and Peel, and countless royalty, dukes and earls. It claims that its bar has never closed in 200 years, a policy which certainly must have lubricated the more extravagant and ill-advised wagers. Current members include Prince Charles and (allegedly) Prince William, and the former held his stag party there in 1981 before marrying Lady Diana Spencer. Despite the fact that his own father had been chairman, Prime Minister David Cameron resigned in 2008 over the Club's refusal to admit women; a stance it maintains to this day. It is said that he is the only person in the history of the club ever to have voluntarily resigned, the usual termination of membership being either death, or being thrown out in disgrace for having brought the reputation of the club into disrepute. This is a notion which may make the rest of us laugh somewhat.

The rampant gambling culture among the wealthy and well-connected, who had both time and money on their hands, is reflected in White's famous Betting Books in which wagers were recorded. It was at White's that an evidently-bored Lord Alvanley allegedly wagered £3,000 (equivalent to a cool quarter of a million in modern currency) on which of two raindrops would reach the bottom of the window pane first, although there is no official record of the bet.

As always, the ruinous habits of the wealthy elite were of considerable interest to the lower orders. *The Connoisseur* was a weekly magazine of sadly short duration (1754–1756), but during its brief life it devoted its May 1754 edition to exposing the goings-on at White's.

One bizarre preoccupation it noted, upon which the members gambled keenly, was death. There was hardly a member or prominent person in the land upon whose mortality very considerable sums were not wagered, and the bets usually pitted one person's life against another's:

> The various changes in the health of one who is the subject of many bets occasion many serious reflections in those who have ventured large sums upon his life or death. Those who would be gainers by his decease upon every slight indisposition watch all the stages of his illness and are as impatient for his death as the undertaker who hopes to have care of his funeral; while the other side are very solicitous about his recovery, send every hour to know how he does and take as great care of him as the clergyman's wife does of her husband, who has no other fortune than his living.

One of the more hopeless wagers on one person outliving another is recorded in the Betting Book of Whites, 1754. Lord Montfort, who was keen on the sort of gambles involving births, marriages and deaths, bet Sir John Bland one hundred guineas that Mr Beau Nash (celebrated dandy) would outlive Mr Colly Cibber (Poet Laureate). Nash was 81, and Cibber was 84, and Lord Montfort had great confidence in Beau's marginal advantage and his ability to cling on to life. Sadly, however, the two gamblers never resolved the wager as they both committed suicide before either Beau or Colly departed this life, and it was gambling debts that drove both men to such desperate ends. Lord Montfort had already lost a fortune at the game of Hazard at White's when he applied for the position of Governor of Virginia, hoping to restore his finances. He didn't get the job. On New Year's Eve he stayed at the club until past midnight, went home, and sent for his lawyer the next morning to put his affairs in order, thus demonstrating some belated responsibility at least. He then went into the next room and shot himself. Sir John Bland managed to lose £32,000 in a single sitting at Hazard, on top of his other considerable losses, thus finally dissipating his entire fortune. He took himself off to France, perhaps to remove himself from temptation, avoid his creditors, and contemplate how to restore his finances. He shot himself in despair on the road from Calais to Paris.

Among the most exalted members of White's was William Augustus, the Duke of Cumberland, who was the third and favourite son of George II. He was also an army general who was despatched by his father to defeat Bonny Prince Charlie's army, which he did at Culloden. The subsequent behaviour of his soldiers however, either ignored or endorsed by him, earned him the nickname of 'The Butcher'. He was also a wildly enthusiastic gambler. When not supervising victorious plundering and mayhem north of the border, he could be found either in the notorious gaming rooms in Bath, or at White's. He was credited with being an ace at Bridge, which may account for his remarkable success in January 1753 when he won a staggering sum estimated to be £255,000 today.

The wonderful *History of White's* (Bourke, 1892) informs us:

We read in the 'Gentleman's Magazine' for January 1753, that his Majesty played at St. James's on 12th Night, for the benefit of the Groom-Porter, and that all the Royal Family were winners. The Duke of Cumberland pocketed £3,000; the losers were the Duke of Grafton, and the Lords Huntingdon, Holdernesse, Ashburnam and Hertford. One is curious to know how the Groom-Porter benefited.

The cost of socialising at the zenith of society was obviously considerable. The noble losers, one assumes, were left with the prospect of explaining their losses to their wives, although at least they did not shoot themselves. 'It will be worth it in the long run, my dear. Trust your husband.'

The duke, as one might suspect from his post-Culloden behaviour, was both a nasty winner and a bad loser. He was responsible for the first major bet on a boxing match between Jack Broughton, the favourite, and Jack Slack, an outsider. The duke bet £10,000 on the favourite at odds of 1:10 and was not pleased at all when a lucky punch from Slack, which virtually blinded Broughton, ended the contest. His Grace immediately set about ruining Broughton by trashing his reputation with imputations of match-fixing, and engineering the closure of the venue from which Broughton earned most of his income. Cumberland, who was obese and had suffered a stroke, died at the age of 44, and one does secretly hope that at least a few members of White's made some money out of his early demise.

Whilst dice games were certainly played by the upper crust, the gentlemen's club members enjoyed card games just as much, probably because of the elements of skill and strategy. The definitive guide for card games was first published in 1742 by Edmond Hoyle, and is still in print today, although considerably expanded as his original remit was the game of Whist, the rudiments of which we are all familiar with from childhood onwards. Basically simple, Whist lent itself to refinement and complexity, skill, strategy, and of course, the games of Solo and Bridge. Serious gamblers could buy texts on probability to give them the edge over their opponents, one of which was the mathematical and erudite *Doctrine of Chances* by Abraham de Moivres, which was first printed in 1718, and is credited with being the first textbook on probability theory in England. Probability theory, in fact, was of interest to many eminent mathematicians over the seventeenth, and particularly eighteenth, centuries. The roll-call of the famous is impressive. Fermat, Pascal, Huygens, Leibnitz, Bayes, de Laplace, Bernoulli and de Moivres were among those brilliant mathematicians who turned their minds to the fascinating problems of chance, and its practical applications. The famous *Pascal's Wager* basically proposed that it made more sense to 'decide' to believe in God because, if He didn't exist and there was no afterlife, then you'd lost nothing. Whereas if He did exist, then you'd improve your chances of going to Heaven, and at little cost to yourself. This reasoning demonstrates some understanding of probability, but none at all about the omnipotence of God, who can apparently see into all human hearts, and would presumably know a chancer when He saw one.

For putative probability experts, games of chance were the perfect vehicle for exploring and expounding their theories. It did not always go well. Gerolamo Cardano, a sixteenth-century polymath, did not personally beggar himself playing games of chance, and indeed was successful enough to just about fund his modest but comfortable lifestyle. Rather suspiciously though, he included a chapter on effective cheating in his famous *Book on Games of Chance* (published posthumously in 1663). However, his younger son stole from his father to fund his own gambling habit, but does not seem to have been either an effective probabilist, or cheat, and had to be disinherited. This was after Gerolamo's elder son had been executed for poisoning his unfaithful wife. Domestic life did not go well for Gerolamo.

Ada, Countess of Lovelace (1815–1852), was the daughter of Lord Byron and an 'amateur' mathematician credited with being the progenitor of computer programming in collaboration with Charles Babbage, the inventor of the Difference Engine. She also put her understanding of probability to work on her quest to design a mathematical model for winning very large bets at horseracing, but with less than happy results. Her obsession with the turf left her thousands of pounds in debt to the syndicate, and her long-suffering husband in despair. She died young, but left a considerable mathematical legacy, even if defeated by the data processing problems of horseflesh.

The definitive modern card gambling game is Poker. It developed as we know it in the nineteenth century, although Georgian gamesters would certainly have been familiar with the forerunners *Poque* (France), or *Pochen* (Germany). The most popular vehicle for gambling in Georgian London clubs, however, was Bridge. Probably after a fine dinner accompanied by copious amounts of alcohol, which some would continue to drink whilst playing, often until dawn, after which they were helped from the premises by liveried but impecunious club servants. The notorious game of Faro should have been one table to be avoided if the members heeded Hoyle's warnings and his assertion that not a single honest Faro bank could be found. That, however, did not stop it being the favourite game of Whig politician Charles James Fox who, by the end of his life, had lost an estimated £200,000 (£17 million) gambling. One would imagine that the best and most successful players would inevitably have been the most abstemious, but such restraint was regarded as slightly suspicious, and possibly even ungentlemanly. Indeed, the vices of alcoholism and chronic gambling seem to have been often inseparable.

To blow away the cobwebs after prolonged nocturnal sessions at White's, Brook's, or Boodle's, however, the members could take to the fresh air to lose even more money.

The upper classes were very keen on horse-racing, as indeed were the lower classes. There were many more racecourses in the eighteenth century than now, although hardly the organised premises we are accustomed to. This was partly because, there being no motorized horse boxes, it was not so easy to get the animals to distant venues, and partly because courses were relatively easy to set up or, indeed, abandon. There are about fifty-nine racecourses operating in England today, and John Cheney mentioned one hundred and twelve in his *Historical List of all the Horse Matches* (1727). Statistics on racecourses which have closed over the last 230 years, however, suggest that this was a considerable underestimate.

The most famous racehorse of all time, Eclipse, was a Georgian. He was born during, and named after, the solar eclipse of April 1764 and his breeder was, unsurprisingly, the Duke of Cumberland. The Duke, of course, died a year later in 1765 and the young Eclipse was sold to a sheep dealer from Smithfield for 75 guineas. This was a fair amount for a yearling of good pedigree, but far less than the amount for which he exchanged hands after he began racing at the age of 5. He started, and won, eighteen races during his career, including eleven King's Plates, and it is estimated that he walked 1,400 miles to meetings throughout England. He had a somewhat high-spirited nature and had the unnerving habit, from the point of view of his jockey, of tearing along with his nose close to the ground. Never having lost a race, he was retired in 1771 after only seventeen months, largely because there was no effective or willing competition. He became a very successful stud and it is known that nearly all English thoroughbred racehorses have Eclipse somewhere in their bloodlines, including the legendary Phalaris, Arkle, Desert Orchid, Kauto Star, and many Derby winners. His skeleton has been preserved (with the addition of the odd hoof or bone from another horse when bits got lost) and is in the Royal Veterinary College near Hatfield. Attempts to discover the reasons for his astounding success have revealed little apparently exceptional, apart from autopsy and skeletal evidence that he had a large heart.

In early Georgian times most horse-races were head-to-head matches of two horses, with the owners wagering against each other, and other gamblers making side bets with each other in 'gentlemen's agreements'. The winners of each head-to-head could then go on to be matched against each other, until a clear victor was declared. Since the whole purpose of horse-racing was to gamble, this system was rather protracted and disorganised and, above all, amateurish. This effectively meant that the 'field' all had the same odds as the ultimate clear winner which we, today, would certainly regard as daft. Horse-racing, moreover, attracted a very wide audience of eager punters, many of whom were in no position to gamble away what little money they had. Authority, of course, was not keen at all on this expansion of the Georgian mania for gambling, and the 1739 Gaming Act was quite explicit about its objections:

'... the Great Number of Horse Races for Small Plates, Prizes or Sums of Money, have contributed very much to the Encouragement of Idleness, to the Impoverishment of the meaner Sort of Subjects of the Kingdom.'

The 'meaner subjects', of course, should have been hard at work in the service of their families and their betters, and not squandering cash on mostly hopeless gambling enterprises involving horseflesh about which they knew little, and possibly with 'gentlemen' who could afford to wager more than they could. True (idle) gentlemen of means were, naturally, largely exempt from this censure since they would not have dreamt of gambling with the lower classes and, anyway, could afford to lose considerable sums without inconveniencing anyone except themselves and their families.

The later development of fields involving more than two horses improved the general excitement and encouraged the habit of the 'gentlemen' to seek each other out by offering odds, but this still needed an anchoring system to become really effective. In the 1790s a man called Harry Ogden realised that this was a waste of a business opportunity, so at Newmarket Heath (close by, but not too close to the organisers and staff), he created the first 'book' offering differing and fixed odds betting on all runners, instead of private wagering. This added considerably to the logic, excitement and prospects, and he is considered England's first known and established bookmaker, although it is probable that others were offering a similar service, but not so successfully. Harry Ogden would seem to have understood both form and probability, and business, and by the nineteenth century the role of the bookmaker was well established.

Racecourses also welcomed the ladies, although they might not have been the racegoers' wives. In *Nana*, a nineteenth-century novel by Emile Zola, the eponymous prostitute heroine with rapacious spending habits, holds court among besotted men with fast-dwindling fortunes at the Longchamps Prix de Paris, there being a filly running which is named after her (which wins, of course). If such things were going on there, they were certainly also going on at English racecourses, and there are reports extant of 'ladies' hiring nearby rooms in which to entertain racegoers of means.

It is, of course, pleasing to contemplate the gambling vices and losses of the wealthy, but less so to think about the poor who also gambled unwisely, and more for reasons of sheer hope and fantasy than reckless and affordable entertainment. The gambling tastes of the upper classes were thus mirrored by those at the lower end of society although, of course, the sums involved were very much smaller, but just as potentially ruinous to those involved. Indeed, the rich and poor often got tangled up together socially while gaming, especially in boxing, and animal-baiting events, as well as horse-racing. As Oliver Goldsmith remarked in his *Life of Beau Nash* (1762) 'Wherever people of fashion came, needy adventurers were found in waiting.'

The main problem with gaming among the poor from the point of view of the religious and civil authorities as we have seen, however, was that they simply could not afford it, and that squandering what little money they had led to starvation, drunkenness and violence, loss of work, child neglect, general despair and – most heinous of all – crimes against the richer and more worthy.

A surprising number of robbers and footpads, who were hanged for their offences, admitted that gaming was at the root of their downfall, including one Joseph Leath who went to the gallows in February 1744. He asked for permission to read a statement to the usual ghoulish crowd as a warning:

Gaming and lewd women will infallibly drag you into practices of a like kind with those for which I suffer. Believe me, every gaming-house is hung with halters, and every one of those wanton creatures, is neither better nor worse, than an agent for the hangman.

It is interesting that he apparently wrote it himself and, if so, he was obviously literate, if not the sort of person who took responsibility for his own actions, at least not until on the scaffold. Many robbers fell into the trap of mugging wealthier citizens and immediately blowing it on drink, gambling and, presumably, those lewd women. This is hardly a surprise considering that any similar lifestyle is also deplored in the twenty-first century media, but at least we do not hang them for it. But in the eighteenth century, as the politician George Savile said in defence of the deterrent effect of the death penalty 'Men are not hanged for stealing horses, but that horses might not be stolen.'

Among the lower classes the most popular entertainments were boxing, games of chance with dice and, of course, cock-fighting. It was not just the poor chickens upon which they wagered though, as the Georgians managed to provoke other animals into vicious bouts, including dogs, bears, and even ducks. Boxing, however, was a much favoured public spectacle for entertainment and wagering, and was particularly noted among the British by their Continental neighbours. Up and down the land, at fairs and in farmyards, in barns and bars, bare-knuckle bouts were being staged and wagers were made. To our minds, it was more like brawling than boxing since this long preceded the 1867 Queensberry Rules about roped rings, timed bouts and intervals, what constituted a knock-out and so forth. Society, however, had been trying to bring some sort of discipline to the 'sport' since the time of the famed Jack Broughton (1704–1789), the Father of English boxing, who devised the 1743 London Prize Ring Rules which went some way towards outlawing wrestling, kicking, eye-gouging, and below-the-belt blows – at least at his own boxing arena which he operated in Hanway Street, London. He also taught boxing skills and devised the 'muffler' which somewhat protected the knuckles from bone-crunching encounters. Later revisions of these rules adopted the square boxing ring of a standard size, and stipulated a rest after a knock-down had ended the round. Previously, spectators sometimes had the highly unedifying habit of dragging groggy fighters to their feet and thrusting them back at their opponents.

Even more alarming than the fighting men were the ferocious women who regularly squared up to each other, often stripped to the waist, which increased their spectacular appeal no doubt.

Such fights were usually between poor women trying to earn a few pence, drew even rougher crowds, and were often held before dawn, such was their notoriety for titillating savagery as the girls risked injury and disfigurement. The cartoonist, Thomas Rowlandson, noted this inversion of gender roles in one of his drawings showing an effeminate dandy rearing away in fright from a pugilistic woman who is squaring up to him with raised fists.

One of the fiercest, and most successful, women fighters was one Elizabeth Wilkinson Stokes. This remarkable woman is not much remembered now since the Victorian penchant for depicting women as gentle and virtuous care-givers preferred to ignore the more robust and physical inclinations of their grandmothers' generation in Georgian times. This was nonsense, of course, but it guided the course of historical record. We do know, however, that Elizabeth was clearly a formidable and considerable athlete – and a big girl, as one male spectator noted nervously. Not only did she fight women, but also took on men, and with weapons such as cudgels, quarter-staffs and short swords. Elizabeth survived her early years of brawling with other women for pitiful money and eventually married Mr Stokes, who owned a prize arena in which she fought. It seems, however, that in the later years of her career – which lasted under a decade, not surprisingly – she preferred some rules. Although willing to pit her skill with weapons against men, when it came to fighting bare-knuckled against women, she promoted the idea of each protagonist holding a coin in her fist and that the first to drop it was the loser. She also devised a 'fighting costume' which maintained some female modesty while allowing freedom of movement. We do not know for certain what ultimately happened to Elizabeth, although she clearly moved upwards in terms of income and fame. One does hope that she retired, had a family, and died an old lady, warm in her bed. Her courage and skills, exercised under awful conditions, should be incorporated in to any modern pantheon of sporting women. And, if it were possible, one might have some questions for Mr Stokes, who was seemingly happy to exploit the safety and welfare of his extraordinary wife for her ability to lure gamblers.

The problem of curbing the enthusiasm of the citizenry for gaming had vexed the authorities for centuries. Henry VIII passed a very comprehensive statute on the issue, which was supplemented in 1730 by additional laws intended, rather hopelessly, to limit the amount of money one could lose at play. This could hardly be enforced successfully against the underclass, and the rich simply ignored it. Justice was further hampered by the fact that the police as we know it did not exist and some magistrates, and their constables, certainly in Westminster and probably nearly everywhere else too, took backhanders to ignore infringements of the gaming laws. In any case, the penalties for being caught were not exactly ferocious and, unless violence was involved, usually meant a fine -which hardly bothered the wealthy – and a promise not to gamble again (which they had no intention of keeping).

In 1751, a somewhat hypocritical Henry Fielding led a raid on a gaming house in The Strand in his capacity as a magistrate, during which forty-five people were arrested and rigged tables were broken up. Fielding, himself, was very partial to a wager. This raid was reported in *The Gentleman's Magazine* as an instance of stiff law-enforcement, and also possibly because no 'gentlemen' were actually involved.

However, attempting to enforce the law could be a very dangerous business for the poor constables (usually dragooned into their duty) as the gamblers in some common gaming houses were often extremely aggressive, attacking them with red hot pokers, knives, swords, tankards, chamber pots, and any other missiles handy. This sort of defiance justified the authorities' belief that many of the denizens were ungentlemanly criminals, even if they did wear swords. In 1721, in a passage off Drury Lane, two constables were killed in a gaming house battle lasting four hours, during which the Riot Act was read and soldiers arrived as reinforcements. That episode resulted in considerable concern among the law-makers.

The Quakers, and other non-conformist groups like the Methodists and Plymouth Brethren, were quick to seize upon the evils of popular vices, and one has to admit that the evidence was all around them. In the poor quarters of towns and cities there were pubs, gambling dens and brothels which all offered opportunities for drinking and gaming, or else there were the streets, markets and fairs. Black Jack of the West (alias of John Blade who was hanged in 1737) was a particularly enterprising rogue, who was a robber and a smuggler. When those occupations spared him some time, he toured the markets and fairs swindling people with illegal and rigged games with evocative names, like Pricking at the Girdle, Old Hat, and the Black Joak. He apparently claimed to have invented and named the latter after a popular, and very bawdy, song of the times. But the devout could be very fundamentalist about the conduct of life:

A testimony against gaming, musick, dancing, singing, swearing, and peoples calling upon God to damn them. As also against drinking to excess, whoring, lying, and cheating. Commended to the consciences of all people in the sight of God, but more especially to those, who keep publick houses.

The struggle against gambling had a long history by the eighteenth century, of course, not least in earlier centuries because it distracted men at times of the week when they were supposed to be doing their compulsory archery practice. During the Civil War and the ensuing Commonwealth, Oliver Cromwell set out some rather dismal strictures against 'pointless' enjoyment, including a definite prohibition on gambling, closing many inns and theatres, imposing dress and conduct rules (especially for women, as usual), and laying down what could be done on a Sunday (church) and what could not be done (work or fun). The concern felt by the eighteenth-century authorities is reflected in the fact that during the 1740s no fewer than four Acts were passed by Parliament to control and regulate gambling, lotteries and horse-racing. The Jockey Club was formed in 1752 by a group of influential gentlemen and set about the organisation and regulation of thoroughbred race meetings and breeding. Tattersall's was established in 1789.

The middle classes, however, were somewhat different. They have always been aspirational in that they want to escape their poorer roots and make their way up the social and financial ladder towards the affluent and influential. For this they depended upon credit, and they were understandably not keen on watching the rich squandering their fortunes at games of Hazard in boozy clubs, instead of investing in worthy commercial enterprise. Besides, many of them would have watched in horror as some undisciplined relative squandered his money and opportunities on vice. This combination of aspiration and propriety has always brought upon the middle classes some derision from both ends of the English social spectrum, but they pegged away with their ambitions and have been responsible for much of the wealth-creation and social opportunity that we have benefited from since. For them, life in the eighteenth century did not generally include habitual gambling, although it is worth mentioning that when the floor of the lawyers' Middle Temple Hall was taken up in about 1764 nearly one hundred pairs of small dice were found among the other bits and pieces which had fallen through the cracks.

To be middle class and respectable, or outwardly at least, meant being law-abiding and God-fearing. The Church of England, back then, generally depended upon the aristocracy for parish livings, so it did not do to rail from the pulpit against such benefactors' more reprehensible behaviour. In fact, clergymen were often rather servile towards the nobility, as Jane Austen skewered in *Pride and Prejudice* in the character of Mr Collins, who was eternally grovelling at the disdainful feet of his patroness, Lady Catherine de Bourgh. The dissenting minister Thomas Shepherd in his *Discourse on Lots* urged his middle-class readers to just accept their situations in life, and not resort to gambling in the vain hope of material improvement: 'Be … Quiet under all the Events of Providence, seeing nothing comes upon thee by Chance; but the Great Sovereign of the World, works all Things after the Counsel of his own Will.'

Indeed, moralists in the eighteenth century became increasingly worried that not only were the aristocratic gamesters betraying their exalted position and political responsibilities, but that they were infecting their inferiors i.e. the aspiring middle classes, who were so valuable to the emerging Empire and economy.

The middle classes and the poor were thus fair game for righteous thundering and general interference. The poor were probably too depressed to take too much notice and did not read anyway, but the middle classes did, and out of Georgian consciences grew the Victorian philanthropists and social activists, many of whom had modest beginnings. It would be a mistake, however, to think that the middle classes were always wreathed in virtue, as common sense (and the worried moralists) suggest that quite a few of those men did, indeed, gamble. In fact, if upwardly mobile and successful men succeeded in breaching the walls of a gentlemen's club, such participation would have been almost inevitable. The prospect of winning money to spend on conspicuous consumption would also have been alluring. A better address, a carriage, more servants, and fi ne clothes and jewellery for the female members of the family might have dangled temptingly in their imaginations, particularly for the daughters upon whom hopes of an advantageous marriage rested. For those who were not eligible for prestigious gentlemen's clubs there were plenty of gaming houses if they fancied a walk on the wild side from time to time. Such places were often remarkably organised, if illegal, and on 7 January 1731 the *Grub Street Journal* published the staff usually employed:

1. A Commissioner, always a Proprietor, who looks in of a night; and the week's account is audited by him and 2 other Proprietors.
2. A Director, who superintends the room.
3. An Operator, who deals the cards at a cheating game called Faroe.
4. Two Crowpees, who watch the cards, and gather the money for the bank.
5. Two Puffs, who have money given them to decoy others to play.
6. A Clerk, who is a check upon the Puffs, to see that they sink none of the money given them to play with.
7. A Squib is a Puff of a lower rank, who serves at half salary, while he is learning to deal.
8. A Flasher, to swear how often the bank has been stript.
9. A Dunner, who goes about to recover money lost at play.
10. A Waiter, to fill out wine, snuff candles, and attend the gaming room.
11. An Attorney, a Newgate Solicitor.
12. A Captain, who is to fight any Gentleman that is peevish for losing his money.
13. An Usher, who lights Gentlemen up and down stairs, and gives the word to the Porter.
14. A Porter, who is generally a Soldier of the Foot guards.
15. An Orderly Man, who walks up and down the outside of the door, to give notice to the Porter, and alarm the house at the approach of the constables.
16. A Runner, who is to get intelligence of the Justices' meetings.

17. Link-boys, Coachmen, Chairmen, Drawers, or others, who bring intelligence of the Justices' meetings, or of the constables being out, at half a guinea reward.
18. Common Bail Affidavit Men, Ruffians, Bravoes, Assassins, cum multis alliis.

Gambling was not, however, the exclusive preserve of eighteenth-century men. Well-bred ladies obviously could not play in the gentlemen's clubs, or common gaming houses, but that does not mean they did not enthusiastically participate in the better class of gaming houses in private residences. Well-known lady gamblers included the beautiful and wayward Georgiana, Duchess of Devonshire. Inevitably, the realisation that women gambled for fun and profit roused particular ire in the moralists since they were supposed to exercise restraint upon their husbands' behaviour (whilst also being obedient); put their families first in all things; and (with the help of religion) fight against any inclination towards vanity, luxury and general moral laxity. Another aspect of female gambling which greatly exercised the virtuous was the question of exactly *how* a female debtor might be forced to honour her obligations if she had no cash or credit left ...

In 1753, a newspaper called *The Prompter*, was particularly venomous:

A Carding WOMAN is a fashionable MONSTER; too Common to be carried about for a Shew, and too Ugly, to bear looking at: Else, there is not, among all the misshapen, grim, Animals, which are proclaim'd UNNATURAL, by Sound of a Trumpet, Any thing, so detestably the Reverse of what she was intended for, as this Rational Grimalkin! this voracious, dry, Harpy, in Masquerade! this, halfhuman, TYGER, in Petticoats!

However, the burden of virtue and example sometimes fell on unwilling female shoulders in Georgian times. Several aristocratic ladies, in particular, were notorious for hosting gaming, one of whom was the Hon. Lady Archer who was a close friend of the Prince Regent, and to whom Thomas Rowlandson dedicated his *Six Stages of Mending a Face* cartoon. She was one of the 'Faro ladies' who concealed the real purpose of the gathering behind a façade such as music or theatricals, and others included Lady Buckinghamshire, Lady Luttrell, and a Mrs Concannon. Being a woman afforded no protection against being raided, though a couple of well-born ladies gamely attempted to claim that being of the peerage rendered them immune from prosecution. Parliament was not impressed, and promptly moved to make the law more explicit and close loopholes. Although the press was usually highly disapproving of gambling women, there was the odd dissenting and supportive voice:

> Dear Ladies of the METROPOLIS, study this PORTRAIT! With the Ladies of PARIS—the moments of improving dissipation are gone by, and a more solid and reasoning character has succeeded to them: but you are in the meridian of what is Ton, Taste, high Play, strict Honor, Faro Tables, Parental Affection, Lottery Insurances, and EXQUISITE SENSIBILITY. To jumble all these qualities properly together, forms at once the character of – a WOMAN OF CAPITAL FASHION! Follow and Embrace it! Be bold! Be desperate!

More often, though, the cartoonists preferred to depict the dreadful consequences of gambling, with the female culprits depicted as ugly, overweight, or in the stocks for their venality.

As bad as the mere venality of gambling, of course, was the roguery and deceit that inevitably attended it. Cheating and game-rigging were rife in eighteenth-century England, mostly although not exclusively, outside the gentlemen's clubs. Dice were loaded, tables physically rigged, cards marked, stooges planted to up the ante, horses nobbled, roulette wheels weighted, odds fixed, tickets forged, and players generally loaded with free or cheap alcohol and, most likely, urged on by those wanton women. Anyone duped by such trickery really should have known better, instead of demonstrating the all-too-human triumph of hope over experience, as it was certainly not new; the brothels of Pompeii, when excavated from beneath the lava of Vesuvius, yielded a good haul of loaded dice.

In the twenty-first century, it is very difficult to cheat in casinos and clubs, due to statistical probability (of which the House is well aware and is tipped in their favour) and electronic surveillance systems. In fact, one does not even need to cheat to get thrown out. Casinos are very disapproving of card-counting, despite the fact that it is legal and a skill, and will ban any player suspected of it, and circulate his or her photograph and details to other casinos.

Not fair? It never was. So the last word will be left to Henry Fielding, that celebrated eighteenth-century magistrate and author who understood, and both loved and loathed, the impulse to gamble, 'That cursed itch of play.' As he said.

Chapter Ten

Learning & The Enlightenment

One problem the time-traveller will have to tactfully cope with is that we know so very much more than the Georgians did, particularly in the realm of natural philosophy as they called it, or science as we now do. Tempting though it might be to hold court in a fashionable salon to explain germs, evolutionary or Big Bang theory, or the quirky aspects of quantum mechanics, this would be unwise. Nobody would believe you, and you might well end up accused of heresy, blasphemy, or even the (theoretically defunct from 1735) 'crime' of witchcraft. All of which could herald unpleasant consequences, whether legal or social. The wise know how to pick their arguments, and it would be very much more useful merely to advocate private, medical and public hygiene in eighteenth-century England. It would also build upon their actual observations and suspicions. To think that the Georgians generally knew less than us in other spheres of learning would be a mistake, however.

Education for the aristocratic and aspiring was, in the eighteenth century, a somewhat rigorous experience by our standards, and began young. It is fair to say that enjoying education, being encouraged to be creative with a paintbrush, learning social skills and having fun, were not general priorities. Some children of wealthy parents were 'home-schooled' by governesses and tutors, but schools were also flourishing, particularly for boys aged seven or over. They tended, however, to focus on grammar and the ancient languages which contributed to modern English, namely Latin, ancient Greek and even Hebrew although less, oddly, on German. The vast vocabulary of modern English is almost two language systems running in parallel with synonyms from each root e.g. *fragile* (French), and *breakable* (Germanic), and thousands of other examples, to which we now ascribe considerable subtlety when choosing which word to use. The Georgians noticed this, and the academic discipline of linguistics was born. Much of this approach was a legacy of the religious educational founders over past centuries. Literacy was, of course, supremely important for any position in a successful life and the way in which men wrote and communicated revealed a great deal to others. It was almost like a code.

You may have noticed that no mention has been made of the education of girls. This, of course, is because except in very enlightened households, this was considered unnecessary. The obviously-undereducated but aspirational Mrs Malaprop in Sheridan's play *The Rivals* (1775) says,

> I would by no means wish a daughter of mine to become a progeny of learning; I don't think so much learning becomes a woman; for instance, I would never let her meddle with Greek, or Hebrew, or algebra, or simony, or fl uxions, or paradoxes, or such inflammatory branches of learning – neither would it be necessary for her to handle any of your mathematical, astronomical, diabolical instruments.

Girls were rigorously schooled in those subjects considered fi t for future wives – such as musical accomplishment and singing, dancing, water-colour painting, embroidery, domestic medicine and the herb garden, religious observance, and general obedience to their menfolk – if they were well-bred. One has to admit that it was quite a curriculum, but it did not foster intellectual or personal freedom. One orphan who did so was Elizabeth Elstob (1683–1756). Her guardian uncle, Charles, thought that female education was largely useless, but nonetheless allowed her to learn Latin and French and have the freedom of his library, of which she made good use. Young Elizabeth, who was clearly much cleverer than her male cousins, was eventually competent in eight languages. One wonders what her uncle thought about all this. Her brother, William, much valued his sister and her intellect, and took her to Oxford, and then London, as his housekeeper. However, he largely just encouraged her educational ambitions and introduced her to his educated friends. She devoted her life to working for, and writing about, women's education, and even influenced Thomas Jefferson. Sadly, however, even she found it difficult to overcome the necessity of a male patron and, after William died in 1715 leaving debts, she was left to fend for herself. Happily, this she managed to do, even in reduced circumstances.

Mary Ann Evans, known to us as the Victorian novelist George Eliot, was born in 1819, so was not really a Georgian herself, as an adult. She did, however, understand the Georgian morality of her own parents and was also largely self-educated. She daringly lived outside marriage with a Mr Lewes for decades and died as his beloved partner, but her greatest novels, such as *Middlemarch*, and *The Mill on the Floss*, are basically Georgian and feature the intelligent but constrained woman or girl chafing against male authority. She, like the Bronte sisters later, chose a pen name which disguised her gender. She opted for a male name, while the later Bronte women chose neutral names – Currer, Ellis and Acton Bell. Over the years it has been suggested many times that their brother, Patrick Branwell Bronte, actually wrote their novels, even though he was an artist and not a writer. He, personally, never suggested any such thing, but it was thought impossible for decent women to conjure up someone like the dangerous Heathcliff. What made it even worse was that their father was a clergyman. He obviously failed as a father and role model considering that his off-spring, isolated in Haworth as they were, gave vent to the febrile imaginations which have so much enriched our literature.

However, education for children began to change in the eighteenth century as can be seen from the number of books specifically published for them, such as William Blake's *Songs of Innocence and Experience* (1789), and *A Pretty Little Pocket-Book* (1744) which was full of games, history and nature study. At the beginning of the 18th century children tended to be viewed as small (and difficult) adults, were dressed in constricting clothing like their parents, and subject to the sort of discipline and religious dogma that we would consider utterly abusive. A Lady Anne Lindsay described her childhood Scottish home as being 'a sort of little Bastille, in every closet of which was to be found a culprit, some sobbing and repeating verbs, others eating their bread-and-water, some preparing themselves to be whipped.'

Dr Isaac Watts (1674–1748), and the 'Father of English hymnody' preferred terrifying children to corporal punishment, as can be seen from his *Divine and Moral Songs for Children*:

> 'Tis dangerous to provoke a God!
> His pow'r and vengeance none can tell.
> One stroke of His almighty rod,
> Shall send young sinners quick to Hell.

Later, however, attitudes softened and moved some way towards the Victorian devotion to childhood and youth which generated so much sentiment, not least in Dickens' novels. The saccharine character of the heroine in *The Old Curiosity Shop* prompted Oscar Wilde to remark that one would have to have a heart of stone not to laugh at the death of little Nell. This veneration of innocence permeated Victorian parlour poetry, popular songs and even advertisements; at a pathetic deathbed of an angelic girl,

'Doctor, must my darling die?'

'There's very little hope, but try Scott's Emulsion.'

The Enlightenment, which was a European phenomenon for most Georgians, actually began in the previous century in terms of published scholarship. Its roots were in a conflict between the organised Christian religions of Catholicism and Protestantism, and scholars who were not at all sure that the churches held all the answers to the social, scientific and philosophical problems that they perceived. All over Europe, from the sixteenth century onwards, literate and learned men were reading more – because they could, thanks to the advancement of printing. And many of them, of course, were literate priests. The roll-call of priests who embraced philosophy and science is considerable and should impress us all, as they often faced real personal danger to defend their studies and conclusions. The institution of the Catholic Inquisition was only finally abolished in the early nineteenth century, after the Napoleonic Wars. It lingers to this day in a more pacifist department of the Vatican named the Congregation for the Doctrine of the Faith which wrestles with modern dilemmas; contraception, abortion, the role of women in the church, the culpability of priests accused of serious misbehaviour, and – somewhat bizarrely – whether unbaptised dead babies must spend time in Limbo before getting into Heaven. Most of us would probably think that babies must be entirely innocent of any sin, whether baptised or not, but others have disagreed. They acknowledged for centuries that tiny infants could hardly be guilty of anything personally, but believed the Biblical assertion that they had been born into a state of original sin which could only be expunged by baptism. This was still of very great concern to Georgian Catholics, and even of some anxiety to some High Church of England Protestants. Only in 2007 did Pope Benedict XVI finally authorise an (unofficial) document which, after years of debate, decided that nobody need agonise any more over the fate of their beloved, unbaptised, and sadly-deceased babies. This, despite the Gospels having given some rather direct instructions on the subject for well over 1,900 years.

But Jesus called the children to him and said, 'Let the little children come to me, and do not hinder them, for the kingdom of God belongs to such as these.' (Luke: 18:16)

Scientifically-minded clergymen in the Enlightenment include the aptly-named Joseph Priestley (1733–1804) who was a scientist, philosopher and rational dissenter from the religious Establishment. Dissenters were believers in God, but did have serious issues with aspects of established Christian doctrine and ritual. Priestley is usually credited with discovering oxygen ('dephlogisticated air') and was a co-founder and minister of the Unitarian Church, but this is only to scratch the surface of his interests, scholarship and achievements. He worked outside London for most of his life but was forced to flee his home in Birmingham after the so-called Priestley Riots in 1791, which were perpetrated over three days in July by a mob who both loathed dissenters, and also believed that they were supporting the French Revolution.

Priestley went first to London, but receiving little support from William Pitt's government, spent the last ten years of his life in Pennsylvania as the Americans, enthusiastically embracing the Enlightenment, had already awarded him a Foreign Honorary Membership of the American Academy of Arts and Sciences in 1782. Anyone wanting to feel the breath leave their body in awe of the sheer scale of this man's interests and achievements should explore his life further although he, himself, paid tribute to the domestic management abilities of his wife, Mary, in enabling him to accomplish so much. It makes one feel rather shame-faced to moan about the much-vaunted pressures of modern life.

Georgian high-achievers were subjected to educational regimes from toddlerhood that we would consider abusive; often combined several jobs or interests as adults; wrote everything they published by hand and probably by candlelight; faced difficulties in communicating with like-minded people, and walked or rode miles in order to do so. These people were tough polymaths. They were also very determined, as many of them believed they were on the cusp of great and far-reaching discoveries. We, on the other hand, are usually confined to a role in a niche sector of science, philosophy or education, because the sheer breadth of our twenty-first century knowledge and interest means that we must specialize. One does suspect that it must have been a lot more fun 250 years ago – at least as an educated and curious adult, with both time and money available.

The Roman Catholic Church is often accused of discouraging or even denying scientific achievement, but that is unfair as it has a distinguished record of natural philosopher priests. Whether or not scientific inquiry was encouraged really depended upon who was Pope at the time. Strangely enough, two of the most conservative popes, who discouraged discussion about topics that might conflict with the word of the Bible, lived in the twentieth century. Some previous popes often seemed very happy to accommodate the investigations of their clever clergy, even if they abjured them to keep their spiritual mission separate from the science. Most of the priest-scientists tried to do so, although sometimes it cannot have been easy, and must have caused some wobbles of faith and allegiance.

One of the best known is the monk Gregor Mendel who, in the nineteenth century, finally established the basic rules of inheritable characteristics thus becoming the 'father' of modern genetics. In 1931, the French priest and physicist Georges Lemaitre published a paper entitled 'The Beginning of the World from the Point of View of Quantum Theory' in the prestigious *Nature* magazine, presaging the Big Bang theory. This must have tested the goodwill of Pope Pius XI, even though he was known for supporting scientific investigation. In the eighteenth century, however, Rene Just Hauy pioneered the discipline of crystallography, which is the arrangement of atoms in a solid. It is unlikely that this much perturbed the Catholic religious hierarchy, even though it actually presaged far greater, and more disturbing, theories. Slightly more alarming would have been the work of the Croatian Roger Boscovich (1711–1787), a Jesuit priest, which was concerned with astronomical matters and largely devoted to correctly determining that the moon had no atmosphere, and a very creditable explanation of the strange orbits of our planets – which mostly went unnoticed by his religious masters. One wonders how he felt about that. Resentment mixed with relief, maybe?

In fact, from the Reformation in the sixteenth century onwards, there was no shortage of eminent Catholic priest-scientists, or even apparently devout Christian laymen. Copernicus (1473–1543) and a Catholic priest, was the first since some ancient Greeks to assert that the sun was the centre of our solar system, rather than the Earth. He was instructed to abandon his heliocentric studies, which he did – at least publicly. Johannes Kepler (1571–1630) was a pious German Lutheran who trained at first for the Ministry, but his inquisitive intellect intervened. He was a brilliant mathematician and astronomer. He had learned about Copernicus and went on to establish his own Laws of Planetary Motion. Galileo Galilei (1564–1642), about whom we all know, was enthusiastic about building upon the astronomical work of his close-contemporaries, but he earned bad marks from Pope Urban VIII, even though the latter originally gave Galileo permission to publish – until the Jesuits and the Inquisition intervened. Most of us, though, credit Galileo with best describing the heliocentric solar system. One rather doubts that he, himself, would have wanted to take all the credit, but he did have a better telescope.

As a visitor to the eighteenth century you may be wondering why the scientific efforts of the previous two centuries are important to anyone trying to blend in and pass themselves off as a Georgian. The reason is that it is very rare that scientific discoveries are truly contemporary to the era to which they are attributed. Some celebrated figures make the historical cut but, behind them, are many people who knew or suspected the same facts but who just did not quite manage to make it into our pantheon of scientific and philosophical heroes. It seems to have taken far longer than most people think for knowledge to become generally accepted. You might personally encounter some of those in the eighteenth century who were at the theoretical cutting edge, and interesting the educated and powerful in their ideas. Or you could encounter the exact opposite; people who did not understand the Enlightenment, and who did a great deal to deny it for religious, or other, reasons.

The great legacy of the Enlightenment is, of course, philosophy. This burgeoned throughout Europe from the sixteenth century onwards, especially in France and England, the foundations being laid by Rene Descartes (1596–1650). Descartes set out to challenge previous thought and authority in the two main areas of knowledge for which he is remembered; philosophy and mathematics. He was hugely influential and turned his attentions to areas previously shunned by thinkers as rather being in the purview of religion, namely The Passions of the Soul, or what we would call emotions. He is remembered most, however, for his reflection on the issue of consciousness *Cogito ergo sum*, I think therefore I am. Great influential philosophers of the eighteenth century include the German Immanuel Kant (1724–1804) who tried to reconcile rational thought with religious belief, individual freedoms, and political authority. Other philosophers who made contributions to modern thought in the areas of politics, economics, the law, and society and the human condition, include David Hume, Adam Smith, Voltaire, John Locke, Thomas Hobbes, Rousseau, and Thomas Paine.

Times of intellectual struggle are always invigorating, interesting, and sometimes dangerous. A mere visitor to the eighteenth century would hardly be likely to embark on a mission of learning, Georgian-style, but would miss out on a great deal of the essence of the era if he or she did not read newspapers and journals, listen in to discussions in coffee shops, and attend public lectures and meetings if possible. Ordinary Georgian workers would hear little about this, of course, but they seem to have had a natural scepticism of Establishment authority which echoed the lofty discourse of their educated 'betters'. It was also their hard and under-educated lives that were so often reflected in the radical philosophical writings which we now consider so seminal. No visitor to Georgian England can abnegate a responsibility to thinking ... whilst also having fun.

Afterword

This has, of necessity, been but a brief tour of some of the more everyday features of living in the eighteenth century, but it is hoped that it has imparted the zest for life that the British Georgians had, and that it has grounded the era in the context of both their predecessor and descendants. They lived in 'interesting times' that were full of contradictions, but nonetheless identifiably *modern*. The wealthier and more educated among them often eagerly embraced capitalism and colonialism, devoured newspapers and journals, established scientific method, applied philosophy to both religion and ethics, sturdily defended individuality and democracy, promoted education, invented the modern novel, and revelled in satire. They certainly had their shortcomings, of course, but then so do we all.

They were somewhat cruel, by our standards. Public executions were both mass entertainment and a ghastly spectacle to deter crime. The poverty stricken or sick were often suspected of being responsible for their own misfortunes, notwithstanding the charity of some paternalistic landowners, and the Parish. Animals were not generally considered to have either feelings or rights, but merely to provide food and entertainment. But … yet … they sowed the seeds of our own more sympathetic, if more complex, society.

Slavery in its strictest sense had never been legal in England after the Norman Conquest, even under feudalism and serfdom, since one human being could not buy another – although one can imagine that quite a few serfs might have found that a rather irrelevant distinction. Those Africans who escaped their abductors into the wider UK were declared legally free, thanks to the Attorney General, Lord Mansfield (1705–1793), who adjudicated in Somersett's Case, 1772, which held that no slave could be forcibly removed from Britain. The earl had little truck with profiteers and Empire-builders when it came to what we would call human rights, and established the principle that slavery did not exist under English law. This effectively emancipated the estimated 10,000 or more 'slaves' in this country, most of whom were in domestic service as black (paid) servants since, however acquired, they were considered rather exotic. Dr Samuel Johnson had an educated black servant from Jamaica called Frances Barber, the son of a slave, whom he made his residual heir after his death, and who inherited Johnson's books, papers, a gold watch, and £70 per annum. Frances was married to a white woman, endured Johnson's eccentric household and way of life, and was loyal and forbearing, but has now all but vanished from history. Joshua Reynolds also had a black servant; it seems it was quite the fashion.

The Georgians lived in the decades during which Africans were being enslaved and transported to the Americas in order to build the wealth of European empires vying for resources and power. We might regret our role in this sorry story, but we were certainly not alone, even if it sometimes sounds like it. Far worse than enduring the yoke of the emerging British Empire was to be under Spanish or Portuguese rule, and even the French and Germans contributed less to infrastructure than we did. We did send soldiers and enforcers, but we also sent administrators and engineers. And, of course, their wives; some of whom may have had a rather different, and possibly influential, perspective on Colonialism.

We might assume today that most Georgians were indifferent to the suffering this caused, but we would be wrong to do so despite the fact that it took from 1772 to 1833 to finally outlaw all aspects of the dismal trade. The assumption that Africa was there for the plundering was reinforced by the fact that the Europeans rarely ventured into the interior to capture slaves personally; they were often sold into slavery by their own chiefs and transported to the western coasts by Arab traders. There, however, they were chained up in the holds of the notorious slave ships in which the conditions are unimaginable and many died. Many Britons, however, were extremely uneasy about the assumption that black people were not of any human value beyond enforced labour. Powerful men, like William Wilberforce, may have trenchantly influenced public opinion, and eventually the law, to great subsequent effect in the nineteenth century, but what about the poor? These were the people who lived in ports such as London, Bristol or Liverpool, who identified with the plight of runaway slaves, hid them in their homes while enforcers searched for them, sometimes subsequently married them, and whose descendants still have a DNA trace in their ancestry, even if there is now little visible evidence. A small, but nonetheless surprising number of white British citizens, have African DNA in their family legacy, which pays tribute to the compassion of the poor. Imagine how you might feel if a desperate, terrified, and fleeing African knocked on your door, begging for sanctuary in a language you could not understand? People did help them, however. The poor did recognise the bereft and desperate, and they certainly knew how venal those British profiteers, who were hunting for the escaped Africans, were. Many of the rich and religious were worried, and said so.

The Georgians, despite the Enlightenment, were also still superstitious. They prayed to the Christian Jesus, but sometimes still hedged their bets by believing in witchcraft, even after the government had declared it false, and Protestant churchmen were disapproving. But before we laugh immoderately at such ideas we should, perhaps, wonder why tabloid newspapers today still feature astrology columns; why we watch television programmes about ghost-hunting; why we are not immune to those who claim to be able to speak to the dead; or why we still attribute an atavistic rightness to books written many centuries or even millennia ago? It could be that we have not progressed so far from eighteenth-century Britain as we would like to think. Humans like to control, or at least influence, their destinies and, when this seems to be a failing ambition, have a tendency to turn to fatalism or superstition.

Atheism is thought to be a modern phenomenon in Europe, but it is not. Philosophers were disputing the existence of gods from the ancients onwards. It had not escaped their notice that powerful rulers were very keen on religion for the purposes of intellectual and civic subjugation, or that the gods were both adaptable and convenient when coercing the general populace into deferential obedience. Roman gods closely mirrored ancient Greek ones, albeit with different names, and the story of Jesus seems to borrow more than somewhat from the story of the Roman Mithras and, indeed, even older legends.

Napoleon, a struggling Catholic believer but also a rationalist, made no bones about it. He reluctantly suspected that religion was but a cynical tool of the powerful which enabled them to manipulate the poor. His closest generals and advisers were secular. Despite his own doubts, however, he also realised the potential for his own regime, 'Religion is excellent stuff for keeping common people quiet. Religion is what keeps the poor from murdering the rich.'

This is not good, but it is a conclusion that has been reached by powerful and ambitious men (and some women) since time immemorial. Only the brave accept their own mortality, that there may be no afterlife, and that it is their own decision whether to be good or not during their brief lifetimes –

entirely due to self-generated moral decisions. The Georgians, or influential ones at least, were prepared to intellectually grapple with these issues as a society. The roll call of eminent Georgians is impressive, and influences us to this day, although they might not be entirely happy with the outcome. We owe a huge intellectual debt to the writers William Congreve, Nicholas Rowe, Laurence Sterne, Tobias Smollett, Voltaire, Jonathan Swift, Daniel Defoe, Henry Fielding, Samuel Richardson, Richard Sheridan, and Samuel Johnson. And to the philosophers David Hume, John Stuart Mill, Jean-Jacques Rousseau, Denis Diderot, Immanuel Kant, Adam Smith, Montesquieu, and their predecessors John Locke, Francis Bacon, René Descartes, and Baruch Spinoza. And to the cartoonists and artists Thomas Rowlandson, William Hogarth, James Gillray and many others. And to the brave scientists who strove to advance the Enlightenment in the footsteps of Isaac Newton and so many others, and who risked their reputations and even their lives to do so. The French guillotined possibly their greatest scientific asset, Antoine Lavoisier – the generally-acknowledged father of modern chemistry – during the Revolution, in 1794. This was because he was a minor aristocrat and a member of the Ferme Générale (tax collector) – a hated profession, for good reasons, but which he only did in order to fund his research. This did not help him sadly.

We even surprisingly owe a considerable debt to some Georgian politicians and judges. Men, such as Lord Mansfield, may have sat in the library in their wealthy homes in front of a cosy fire, but they were often thinking uneasily about the poor, the disadvantaged, and ethics.

And these people are only a few of the most famous. The least we can do, given our hubristic notions of our own knowledge and morals, is to learn about them and the common people they tried to either help or celebrate. They are all long gone now. But these Georgians bequeathed a great deal to us during an exciting time to be alive, often did manage to have great fun while they were here, and still influence us to this day.

If I have to leave a last notion, then it is to not judge our eighteenth century forebears on modern principles and social media chatter, despite the fact that, had they had the opportunity, they would all have been undoubtedly tweeting away like mad.

Sometimes, less communication translates to more thinking. The Georgians did a lot of thinking.

Acknowledgements

I would first like to thank my niece and fellow-author, Catherine Curzon (aka 'Madame Gilflurt'), who has encouraged and helped me considerably, not to mention prising me out of the house to go to the theatre, and performances such as *An Evening with Jane Austen*, which is a wonderful medley of readings and music, and a delight for any Regency buff.

I must also acknowledge those tireless and enthusiastic historians and researchers, whether professional, academic, or amateur, who share their knowledge online, and who are often such a great source of primary documentation. Individuals include Mike Rendell, Madame Gilflurt, Rosemary Sweet (et al), Polly Bull, Steve Poole, and so many others that I cannot even begin to acknowledge them, save some in the Bibliography. But they are out there, if you care to look.

The Universities of Harvard, Toronto, Bath, London, Bristol, South Carolina, and York, among others, have been invaluable resources. As have been the British Library, the records of the proceedings of the Old Bailey, the London Museum, the Hunterian Museum, the British Museum, and the Library of Congress. To any others upon whose expertise I have depended, but whom I fail to mention in person here, I can only apologise and hope that I have included almost everyone in the Endnotes and Bibliography. Tracking knowledge online is easier these days in one respect, but more difficult in others.

I also would like to thank cousin Frances and friend Bob, who volunteered their considerable editing expertise and intellect, but did not always get the opportunity to exercise their skills, entirely due to my rather haphazard method of writing. They did their best and never complained.

Finally, I would like to acknowledge the support of my two beloved sons. Ben who, when informed I was writing a book about Georgian England, just burst out laughing and told me that nobody would ever buy it. He's a chef. And James, who was rather more upbeat, but just kept nagging about progress – dear lad. He works in digital advertising with *deadlines....*

Chapter Notes and Website References

Chapter 1: How to be a Georgian
The East India Company which built the British Empire
http://www.bl.uk/learning/histcitizen/trading/story/company.html

Non-Conformism (Dissenters) from the sixteenth century onwards
http://www.encyclopedia.com/history/modern-europe/british-and-irish-history/dissent

Timeline of eighteenth century British newspapers
http://www.bl.uk/reshelp/findhelprestype/news/concisehistbritnews/britnews18th/

Historical maps of London's development
http://www.oldmapsonline.org/en/London,_United_Kingdom

The evolution of mealtimes
http://www.bbc.co.uk/news/magazine-20243692

Chapter 2: Clothes & Beauty
The 'Macaronis'
http://rictornorton.co.uk/eighteen/macaroni.htm

William Hogarth – *The Rake's Progress*
http://www.tate.org.uk/whats-on/tate-britain/exhibition/hogarth

Getting dressed (toffs and commoners)
https://www.youtube.com/watch?v=yMy15UMgcgAg
https://www.youtube.com/watch?v=Ggvvr_l-U2Q

How to do the Versailles Glide
http://leslie-carroll.blogspot.co.uk/2009/08/versailles-glide.html
https://www.youtube.com/watch?v=VYw9b6clIMs

Thomas Rowlandson's cartoon of *Six Stages of Mending a Face*
http://www.metmuseum.org/art/collection/search/392701

William Pitt breaking the news of the shooting of the king of Sweden to George and Caroline
https://62e528761d0685343e1c-f3d1b99a743ffa4142d9d7f1978d9686.ssl.cf2.rackcdn.com/files/83410/area14mp/image-20150529-15221-1kqg7u6.jpg

The bourdaloue
https://janeaustensworld.files.wordpress.com/2012/07/francois_boucher__la_bourdaloue_01b.jpeg

Chapter 3: Home & Work
The cost of living
https://www.oldbaileyonline.org/static/Coinage.jsp

Women's jobs in the eighteenth century
http://www.history.ac.uk/reviews/review/708a

Science in the eighteenth century
http://www.daviddarling.info/encyclopedia/S/science_in_the_eighteenth_century.html

How to build a canal
https://en.wikipedia.org/wiki/Canal

Social work and welfare in the eighteenth century
https://www.history.ac.uk/ihr/Focus/welfare/articles/shaves.html

Aspirational middle class life at home
https://www.bl.uk/romantics-and-victorians/articles/the-middle-classes-etiquette-and-upward-mobility

Chapter 4: Health & Medicine
Medicinal recipes from the eighteenth century with ingredients which may be hard to source or not very appealing
https://18thcenturyrecipes.wordpress.com/category/18th-century-medical-recipes/

The role of the barber-surgeon
https://thechirurgeonsapprentice.com/2010/09/15/surgeons/

The French father of modern dentistry, Pierre Fauchard, to whom we should be grateful
http://www.jdao-journal.org/articles/odfen/pdf/2011/01/odfen2011141p103.pdf

Medical procedures and instruments from the eighteenth century which strike fear into the heart
https://18thcenturyminds.wikispaces.com/Medical+Procedures+and+Medications

The Unmentionable: venereal disease in all its horror
http://sloaneletters.com/suffering-venereal-disease-in-the-early-eighteenth-century/

The health of seamen in the Royal Navy, a source of considerable medical advance (P.K. Crimmin (1999) 'The sick and hurt board and the health of seamen C. 1700–1806', *Journal for Maritime Research*, (1:1, 48–65)
http://www.tandfonline.com/doi/pdf/10.1080/21533369.1999.9668299

Fanny Burney's Mastectomy: The Faber Book of Reportage,   Carey, J , Faber & Faber, London (1996).

Chapter 5: Fitness & Sport
Health-giving cold baths and plunge pools for the rich in the eighteenth century
http://www.buildingconservation.com/articles/bath-houses/bath-houses.htm

London's first public swimming bath – the Peerless Pool
https://janeaustensworld.wordpress.com/2009/03/04/the-peerless-pool-londons-first-outdoor-public-swimming-pool/

Boxing, for both men and women
http://www.fscclub.com/history/fame-prize-e.shtml

'Sporting Days in Eighteenth Century England' (Brailsford, D., 1982, *Journal of Sport History*, Vol 9, No 3)
http://library.la84.org/SportsLibrary/JSH/JSH1982/JSH0903/jsh0903d.pdf

How to vault over a bull in Knossos, with useful diagram.
http://travelingclassroom.org/?p=124

Chapter 6: Behaving Properly
Eighteenth century etiquette and expectations
https://loversandliarsmedley.wordpress.com/about/a-dramaturgs-perspective/18th-century-ettiquette-expectations/

The great importance of dancing (Fawcett, T., *Dance and Teachers of Dance*, Bath University)
https://www.bathspa.ac.uk/Media/CHC%20Images/Vol%2002%20-%2002.%20Fawcett%20-%20Dance%20and%20Teachers%20of%20Dance%20in%20Eighteenth-Century%20Bath.pdf

How to dance the Gavotte
https://www.youtube.com/watch?v=DKOXVE_pskA

Chapter 7: Law & Order
Crime and punishment in Georgian Britain (Matthew White, British Library)
http://www.bl.uk/georgian-britain/articles/crime-and-punishment-in-georgian-britain

'The London Mob: Violence and Disorder in Eighteenth Century England' (Patrick Dillon, *History Today*)
http://www.historytoday.com/patrick-dillon/london-mob

'Crime, Poverty and Social Policy in the metropolis' (*London Lives*); a tremendous resource for all aspects of eighteenth-century life
https://www.londonlives.org/static/Background.jsp

Chapter 8: A Night at the Opera
Scurrilous eighteenth-century fun
https://gerryco23.wordpress.com/2014/07/25/city-of-laughter-bawdy-and-scurrilous-18th-century-london/

The rise of the 'Penny Dreadful' – popular 'literature' in an age of increasing literacy
https://historicromance.wordpress.com/2010/07/07/saucy-rude-and-crude-the-18th-century-chapbook/

David Garrick, the father of modern theatre
https://www.garrickclub.co.uk/david_garrick/

The 1891 biography of the 'Gifted Amateur', Robert Coates, aka 'Romeo', 'Diamond' or 'Curricle Coates', (Robinson, J. R. & Robinson, H. H., University of Toronto archive)
https://archive.org/details/lifeofrobertcoat00robiuoft

Chapter 9: Gambling
Gamblers, Cheats and Fatalists: On Books, Streets, and Migrant Footsteps (Harskamp, J., & Dijstelberg, P., Wordpress, 2012)
https://abeautifulbook.wordpress.com/2012/05/13/gamblers-cheats-and-fatalists/

Gambling in London's Gentlemen's Clubs (Luke Rees)
https://londonhistorians.wordpress.com/2014/06/05/gambling-in-londons-most-ruinous-gentlemens-clubs/

Eighteenth-century horse racing
http://mikerendell.com/18th-century-horse-racing/

'Whist is boring': *Historic Card Games* (David Parlett)
http://www.davidparlett.co.uk/histocs/

How to play Hazard, at your own risk.
http://dicegames.org/hazard/

Chapter 10: Learning & The Enlightenment
Popular politics in the eighteenth century (White, M., British Library)
https://www.bl.uk/georgian-britain/articles/popular-politics-in-the-18th-century

The European Enlightenment (Encyclopaedia Britannica)
https://www.britannica.com/event/Enlightenment-European-history

The Enlightenment and science: ' What was the Enlightenment?', Szalay, J., *Live Science* (2016)
http://www.livescience.com/55327-the-enlightenment.html

A dubious schoolboy lifestyle …
https://lifetakeslemons.wordpress.com/2011/06/15/portrait-of-an-english-schoolboy/

Select Bibliography

Primary Sources

Beattie, J.M., *The First English Detectives: The Bow Street Runners and the Policing of London, 1750–1840* (Oxford University Press, 2012)

Berkovitz, Barry K.B., *Nothing but the Tooth: A Dental Odyssey* (Newnes, 2012)

Blake, W., *Songs of Innocence and Experience: Shewing the Two Contrary States of the Human Soul*, 1780 (Oxford University Press, 1970)

Brown, M., *Performing Medicine: Medical Culture and Identity in Provincial England, c.1760–1850* (Manchester University Press, 2011)

Chill, Adam, *Boundaries of Britishness: Boxing, Minorities, and Identity in Late-Georgian Britain* (ProQuest, 2007)

Crego, R., *Sports and Games of the 18th and 19th Centuries* (ABC-CLIO, Westport USA, 2003)

Cruickshank, D., *London's Sinful Secret: The Bawdy History and Very Public Passions of London's Georgian Age* (St. Martin's Press, 2010)

Durston, Gregory J., *Whores and Highwaymen* (Waterside Press, 2012)

French, Dr R. & Cunningham, Dr A. (Eds), *The Medical Enlightenment of the 18th Century* (Cambridge University Press, 2014)

Harvey, K., *The Little Republic: Masculinity and Domestic Authority in Eighteenth-Century Britain* (Oxford University Press, 2012)

Hope, R., *Poor Jack – the Perilous History of the Merchant Seaman* (Chatham Publishing, London, 2001)

Jackson, G. and Ludlow, C., *A Grim Almanac of Georgian London* (The History Press, 2013)

Laurence, A., *Women in England, 1500–1760: A Social History* (Phoenix Press, London, 1994)

McLynn, F., *Crime & Punishment in 18th Century England* (Routledge, Oxon, 1989)

Norton, R., *Mother Clap's Molly House: The Gay Subculture in England, 1700–1830* (Chalford Press, 2006)

Pearson, R., 'The impact of fire and fire insurance on eighteenth century English town buildings and their populations', *Investing in the Early Modern Built Environment: Europeans, Asians, Settlers and Indigenous Societies*, ed. by Carole Shammas (BRILL, 2012)

Porter, R., *The Penguin Social History of Britain: English Society in the 18th Century* (Penguin Books Limited, London, 1990)

Rendell, M., *Astley's Circus – the story of an English Hussar* (Createspace Independent Publishing Platform, 2013)

Robins, N., *The Corporation that Changed the World: How the East India Company Shaped the Modern Multinational* (Pluto, London, 2006)

Robinson, J. H. & H. H., *Life of Robert Coates* reprinted 2007 by Kesinger Publishing, LCC.

Saxton, K.T., *Narratives of Women and Murder in England, 1680–1760: Deadly Plots* (Ashgate Publishing, 2009)

Schliefer, E. & Temple, R., *The Compulsive Gambler* (Xlibris, USA, 2009)

Smith, D.F. & Lawhon, M.L., *Plays about the Theatre in England 1737–1800, of the Self-Conscious Stage from Foote to Sheridan* (Bucknell University Press, Lewisburg, 1979)

Stack, S., *The Whole Duty of a Woman: or, an Infallible Guide to the Fair Sex* (1737), Harvard University Library.

Steele, V., *The Corset, A Cultural History* (Yale University Press, Newhaven and London, 2001)

Ward, Richard M., *Print Culture, Crime and Justice in 18th-Century London* (Bloomsbury Publishing, 2014)

Wild, A., *The East India Company: Trade and Conquest from 1600* (The Lyons Press, New York, 1999)

Secondary Sources

Beattie, J.M., 'Sir John Fielding and Public Justice: The Bow Street Magistrates' Court, 1754–1780', *Law and History Review*, 25:1 (2007)

Boulton, J., 'Welfare Systems and the Parish Nurse in Early Modern London, 1650–1725', *Family & Community History*, 10:2 (2007)

Chater, K., 'Black people in England, 1660–1807', *Parliamentary History*, 26:S1 (2007)

Devereaux, Simon, 'England's "Bloody Code" in Crisis and Transition: Executions at the Old Bailey, 1760–1837', *Journal of the Canadian Historical Association/Revue de la Societe historique du Canada*, 24:2 (2013)

Draper, N., 'The City of London and slavery: evidence from the first dock companies, 1795–1800', *The Economic History Review*, 61:2 (2008)

Erickson, A.L., 'Married women's occupations in eighteenth-century London', *Continuity and Change*, 23:02 (2008)

Fulford, T., 'Fallen Ladies and Cruel Mothers: Ballad Singers and Ballad Heroines in the Eighteenth Century', *The Eighteenth Century*, 47:2 (2007)

Harvey, K., 'Barbarity in a Teacup? Punch, Domesticity and Gender in the Eighteenth Century', *Journal of Design History*, 21:3 (2008)

Haycock, D.B. & Wallis, P., 'Quackery and commerce in seventeenth-century London: the proprietary medicine business of Anthony Daffy', *Medical History. Supplement* (2005)

Laughran, M., 'History of Fashion from Head to Toe: Cosmetics from Ancient Times to the Present Day', *Aspects of American Culture Series*, Saint Joseph's College of Maine (2003)

Manley, K.A., 'The Road to Camelot: Lotteries, the Circle of Learning, and the "Circulary" Library of Samuel Fancourt', *The Library*, 8:4 (2007)

McTaggart, P & A., 'Ease, Convenience and Stays, 1750–1850', *Costume* 13, 41–51 (1979)

Rabin, Dana Y., 'Seeing Jews and Gypsies in 1753', *Cultural and Social History*, 7:1 (2010)

Shoemaker, R.B., 'The Street Robber and the Gentleman Highwayman: Changing Representations and Perceptions of Robbery in London, 1690–1800', *Cultural and Social History*, 3:4 (2006)

Smith, C.W., '"Callico Madams": Servants, Consumption, and the Calico Crisis', *Eighteenth-Century Life*, 31:2 (2007)

Tosney, N., 'Legacies of seventeenth-and eighteenth-century gaming in modern attitudes towards gambling' *Community, Work & Family*, 13:3 (2010)

Turner, D.M., 'Popular marriage and the law: Tales of bigamy at the eighteenth-century old Bailey', *London Journal*, 30:1 (2005)

Wright, L., 'Street Addresses and Directions in Mid-Eighteenth Century London Newspaper Advertisements', *News discourse in early modern Britain: selected papers of CHINED 2004* (2006)

Archives
The Proceedings of the Old Bailey, Law Society Archive

Index